The Evangelical and The Open Theist

Can Open Theism Find Its Place Within The Evangelical Community?

Garrett Ham

Copyright © 2014 Garrett Ham

All rights reserved.

ISBN: 978-1496192301

All scriptural quotations, unless otherwise indicated, are taken from the Holy Bible, New International Version®. Copyright © 1973, 1978, 1984, 2011 by Biblica, Inc.™ Used by permission of Zondervan. All rights reserved worldwide. www.zondervan.com. The "NIV" and "New International Version" are trademarks registered in the United States Patent and Trademark Office by Bilica, Inc.™

Scripture quotations identified NASB are taken from the New American Standard Bible®, Copyright © 1960, 1962, 1963, 1968, 1971, 1972, 1973, 1975, 1977, 1995 by the Lockman Foundation. Used by permission. (www.Lockman.org)

Scripture quotations identified NRSV are taken from the New Revised Standard Version Bible, Copyright © 1989, Division of Christian Education of the National Council of the Churches of Christ in the United States of American. Used by permission. All rights reserved.

Scripture quotations identified KJV are from the King James Version of the Bible.

Scripture quotations identified as NLT are taken from the Holy Bible, New Living Translation, copyright ©1996, 2004, 2007, 2013 by Tyndale House Foundation. Used by permission of Tyndale House Publishers, Inc., Carol Stream, Illinois 60188. All rights reserved.

CONTENTS

PREFACE 1

1 INTRODUCTION 5
The Evangelical Understanding of Scripture 5
The Nature of Scripture 6
The Purpose of Scripture 7
The Authority of Scripture 9
Basics of Open Theology 10
Book Objective 12

2 SCRIPTURE 19
Questioning Exhaustive Divine Foreknowledge 19
Divine Repentance 19
   (i) Exodus 32:7-14 19
   (ii) Jeremiah 18:7-10 25
   (iii) The Book of Jonah 26
   (iv) Other passages 27
The Divine Perhaps 29
The Divine If 31
The Divine Consultation 33
The Divine Question 34
Hermeneutical Fallacies 36
Affirming Exhaustive Divine Foreknowledge 42
1 Samuel 15:29 42
Numbers 23:19 44
Psalm 139 45
Isaiah 40-55 46
Prophecy 46
Peter's Denial 50
The Predestined and the Elect 50
Romans 9-11 51
Conclusion 65

3 PHILOSOPHY AND SYSTEMATICS 79
A Paradigm Shift 79
Divine Immutability 79
Divine Impassibility 81

Divine Foreknowledge 83
    (i) Denying omniscience? 83
    (ii) The futility of foreknowledge 85
    (iii) Issues of time and timelessness 86
Divine Sovereignty 90
    (i) General Sovereignty 90
    (ii) Predestination 93
    (iii) Metasovereignty 93
Practical Implications 94
    Prayer 94
    Providence 95
    Theodicy 97
Conclusion 98
4 CONCLUSION 105
  Compatible Schools of Thought? 105
  Defining Systematics 106
  Conclusion 108
BIBLIOGRAPHY 111
ABOUT THE AUTHOR 119

PREFACE

The interaction between God and man in Scripture has always been of great interest to me. I find the Bible's depictions of these dynamic encounters of mutual influence striking in their refusal to cohere with our neat theological systems. Disregarding our desire for an easily comprehensible picture of the divine, devoid of complexity and nuance, these narratives portray a God besieged by a disobedient and insolent people that nevertheless remain the object of his affections. The ability of the human players to influence divine action is particularly thought provoking.

Standing in contrast to the one-dimensional teachings about God to which I had grown accustomed, I found myself repeatedly drawn to these narratives while completing my theological studies at Ouachita Baptist University. I therefore naturally focused my research on the philosophical and theological debates to which these narratives gave rise.

Studying these matters within an evangelical academic setting made it impossible to avoid the dispute then raging between traditional and open theists. I was fixated and decided to focus my senior thesis on the topic. What follows is the result of my research.

It has been seven years since I graduated from Ouachita, and I have only now decided to make my research publicly available. As I do so, however, I feel I must preface the work that follows with the following points.

First, I do not claim to be a biblical scholar or theologian. As I write this preface, I am an attorney, and, despite having written this book prior to the completion of my legal studies, its contents nonetheless reflects the basic mindset of an attorney. Which is to say, my interest lies more in the strength of each side's arguments than the merits of one position over another.

My original purpose in writing this book was to explore whether open theism and evangelicalism are—as many have claimed—mutually exclusive.

To do so, I had to assume the foundational beliefs of evangelicalism and then evaluate the arguments of open theism in their best light. This is important to keep in mind while reading through my work, as its purpose is not to establish the open model of God as the correct one, but rather to establish that its proponents have a legitimate claim to the title "evangelical."

Second, as I suggested above, this book is not a treatise in support of open theism. While I am sympathetic to the movement and its attempts to refocus evangelicals away from the writings of the Reformers and their successors and back onto Scripture, I eventually came to reject this school of thought. Plainly put, I am not an open theist, and I find its claims presumptuous and unpersuasive.[1]

Indeed, I view with suspicion any theological system makings its initial appearance centuries after the apostolic age—which includes both open theism and Calvinism. I hope that modern proponents of traditional theism, with its long and rich theological heritage, will produce more compelling and thoughtful counterarguments against open theism than the frankly embarrassingly superficial works that have thus far littered the theological landscape.

Nevertheless, my reservations regarding open theism notwithstanding, arguing for a compatibility between open theism and evangelical theology is quite different from affirming the assertions of open theology. Without an understanding of this book's real purpose, it will be easy to believe that I am arguing in favor of open theism, but that is simply not the case.

An honest evaluation of another point of view requires us to reflect upon it in its best possible light and to consider its proponents' arguments as they make them, not as we would frame them in light of our opposition to the conclusions presented. Sadly, too many opponents of open theism have fallen into this trap, setting up straw men and thereby undermining their own position. This is demagoguery, not debate, and I am loath to see theological discourse reduced to the level of political theater.

Third, this book was originally written as an undergraduate thesis, and its purpose is therefore not to make a significant scholarly contribution to theological studies, as a doctoral dissertation might. Indeed, as I edited this book to strengthen some areas of weakness, I did so through the eyes of an attorney, not a scholar. Nevertheless, I believe this book presents a fairly comprehensive evaluation of current sources and arguments that should serve as a good jumping-off point for those wishing to explore the subject further.

Finally, I must note that I have made only minor modifications to this work since it originally appeared in the library of Ouachita Baptist University under its original name *A Scriptural and Philosophical Evaluation of the Open Model of God as an Ontological Necessity and Its Compatibility with Evangelical The-*

ology. I made some revisions in light of my removing it from a purely academic environment, the most obvious of which is the name, but other revisions appear throughout as well.

For example, I originally wrote this book assuming the audience had a basic understanding of Greek and Hebrew. I edited this book without that assumption. So, while I retained analysis of the original languages and issues in translation where appropriate, I rewrote these sections with more explanation for those unacquainted with the languages and removed quotes from the original manuscripts. I also fleshed out theological terms and concepts that I previously left unexplained.

Most other changes, however, are relatively minor. I strengthened some arguments I found weak and corrected some typographical errors and awkward phrasing present in the original work. While the arguments are somewhat underdeveloped, I believe this short volume effectively and succinctly describes and analyzes the abundance of applicable authorities and arguments currently available. I hope eventually to rewrite and expand this work in light of the research and study I have conducted since graduating from Ouachita, but that will have to wait for another time.

I decided to make this work available now, as it is currently written, so that it could potentially serve as a guide for those who want to dive deeper into the controversy surrounding open theism and its impact on the evangelical community and, indeed, the evangelical understanding of God and his purposes in the world. I hope this work is of value for you in your studies, whether personal or academic.

Endnotes

[1] In light of the great depth of theological thought encompassing two millennia of Christian belief and practice, I find the debate surrounding open theism to be particularly superficial. The dispute itself seems to me to be an undeveloped expression of an immature movement—immature in the sense that, relative to Christianity as a whole, evangelicalism is a recent expression of the faith. While the modern appearance of open theism as a developed theological system does not necessarily undermine the answers the movement seeks to offer, it does, in my opinion, undercut the very questions both it and its opponents are asking. I believe we could learn a lot from the Eastern Church's understanding of mystery. While I believe open theism to provide an adequate if somewhat shallow view of God as he relates to humanity, attempts to describe with certainty the divine essence in terms of theological systems—indeed, in any concrete terms at all—seems to me a foolhardy endeavor.

1 INTRODUCTION

The story of evangelicalism is one of complex theological development and expression. Through the years, the term evangelical has carried a wide range of meanings.[1] While modern evangelicalism is by no means a monolithic movement, across the spectrum its foundational beliefs lie in its affirmation of three major theological principles:

> (1) the complete reliability and final authority of Scripture in matters of faith and practice; (2) the necessity of a *personal* faith in Jesus Christ...and (3) the urgency of seeking actively the conversion of sinners to Christ.[2]

The first principle is the most pertinent to the question at hand, though the implications of open theism touch on the second and third principles as well.

The Evangelical Understanding of Scripture

The great diversity among evangelicals makes any effort to define the evangelical view of Scripture quite difficult. Realizing this, evangelicals have at various times come together to formulate statements of faith distinctive enough to differentiate themselves from other groups—such as Roman Catholics, Eastern Christians, and liberal Protestants—but broad enough to leave the interpretation of such statements to the individual.

InterVarsity Christian Fellowship's affirmation of the "unique divine inspiration, entire trustworthiness and authority of the Bible," for example, leaves great room for interpretation, typical of many such attempts to define evangelical bibliology.[3] While there may be disagreements among evangelicals regarding terminology, such as the meaning of "divine inspiration," "entire trustworthiness," and "authority of the Bible," the common strand binding all evangelicals together is a high view of the authority and reliability of Scripture in matters of faith.[4]

Yet, recent years have witnessed a debate over who can legitimately claim the title "evangelical." Issues ranging from evolution to conditional immortality have forced evangelicals to reevaluate where to draw the line between evangelicalism and broader Christian thought. Nowhere has this trend more clearly manifested itself than in the intense, emotionally charged debate surrounding open theism.

Yet the difficulty associated with defining the term "evangelical" compounds the difficulty associated with determining evangelicalism's compatibility with all but the most blatantly unorthodox Protestant theologies. Consequently, determining the place—or lack thereof—of open theology within the evangelical tent requires the establishment of a basic understanding of what it means to be an evangelical.

Evangelicals readily agree that they hold a high view of Scripture. What constitutes a high view of Scripture, however, is a matter open to debate; and yet in order to evaluate properly the legitimacy of open theism as an evangelical school of thought, a basic understanding of the evangelical view of Scripture is essential.

Therefore, in this chapter, I will outline the basic evangelical approach to Scripture in order to assess its compatibility with open theism.[5] The best way to grasp the evangelical understanding of the Christian Scriptures is to evaluate how self-professing evangelicals have themselves defined that understanding.

The Nature of Scripture

At the core of evangelical theology lies a distinct understanding of the character of Holy Scripture. Christianity Today International affirms that the "sixty-six canonical books of the Bible as originally written were inspired of God, hence free from error." Article VII of the Chicago Statement on Biblical Inerrancy states that "inspiration was the work in which God by His Spirit, through human writers, gave us His Word. The origin of Scripture is divine."

Article IX goes on to affirm that

> inspiration, though not conferring omniscience, guaranteed true and trustworthy utterance on all matters of which the Biblical authors were moved to speak and write...[we deny] that the finitude or fallenness of these writers, by necessity or otherwise, introduced distortion or falsehood into God's Word.

The very phrase "authority of scripture," is a "shorthand way of saying that, though authority belongs to God, God has somehow invested this authority in scripture."[6]

Article XI of the Chicago Statement on Biblical Inerrancy, adequately summarizing the consensus evangelical view, affirms "that Scripture, having been given by divine inspiration, is infallible, so that, far from misleading us, it is true and reliable in all the matters it addresses."[7]

Finally, the Evangelical Theological Society, the most visible battleground in the traditional-openness debate, summarizes the broad evangelical view regarding the nature of Scripture: "The Bible alone, and the Bible in its entirety, is the Word of God written and is therefore inerrant in the autographs."

The Purpose of Scripture

Since the first century, Christians have affirmed Scripture as the signpost pointing the way to salvation.

> You are contentious, brethren, and zealous for the things which lead to salvation. You have studied the Holy Scriptures, which are true, and given by the Holy Spirit. You know that nothing unjust or counterfeit is written in them (1 Clement 40:1-3).

This historic understanding of Scripture plays an important role in evangelical theology because at the heart of evangelicalism is the effort to maintain what evangelicals view as the historic faith. This becomes particularly understandable in light of nineteenth-century German liberalism and the attempts to "demythologize" the Bible by theologians such as Rudolph Bultmann.

To evangelicals, Scripture stands as the invariable keeper of the apostolic teaching. Evangelicals do not view themselves as a twentieth century phenomenon but rather as defenders of the two-thousand-year-old teachings of Christ and his apostles. Evangelicals understand their faith to be firmly rooted in what they believe to be "historic or biblical Orthodoxy."[8]

Modern evangelicals echo the call of Clement of Rome. Although it is their view of Scripture that generally distinguishes them from other schools of Christian thought, salvation by faith in Christ is the fundamental tenet of evangelical theology.[9] To the evangelical, Scripture is the infallible guide directing humanity to salvation.

The Westminster confession affirms the "full discovery [Scripture] makes of the only way of man's salvation."[10] The Tyndale University College and Seminary asserts that "through the power of the Holy Spirit, God speaks to us in the Scriptures today to accomplish his purpose of salvation in Jesus

Christ." The 1st summary of the 1978 Chicago Statement on Biblical Inerrancy is less oblique:

> God, who is Himself Truth and speaks truth only, has inspired Holy Scripture in order thereby to reveal Himself to lost mankind through Jesus Christ as Creator and Lord, Redeemer and Judge. Holy Scripture is God's witness to Himself.

Scripture is the ultimate means to salvation, for it is through Scripture that people encounter the claims of Christ and their implications for daily life.[11]

Trinity Evangelical Divinity School believes the

> Scriptures, both Old and New Testaments, to be the inspired Word of God, without error in the original writings, *the complete revelation of his will for the salvation of men*, and the Divine and final authority for all Christian faith and life (emphasis added).

Clause 2 of the 1974 Laussanne Covenant, a declaration of European evangelical faith, affirms the "power of God's Word to accomplish his purpose of salvation." The Japan Bible Seminary argues that Scripture "contains all that God pleased to reveal to men concerning salvation."

The common theme running throughout evangelical expressions of bibliology is the idea of the Bible's place as the written revelation of God for the salvation of man. "In every age and every place, this authoritative Bible, by the Spirit's power, is efficacious for salvation through its witness to Jesus Christ."[12]

This understanding of Scripture and authority, however, introduces ambiguity into the formation of systematic theology. That is to say, if Scripture exists to bring men to saving grace, as the typical evangelical will affirm, then where Scripture is ambiguous or unclear on matters of doctrine, there is room for various interpretations. This opens the door for theological diversity within the evangelical community.

Of course, there is a limit to the diversity evangelical theology can tolerate. Obviously, Arianism and Mormonism are excluded, as well as alternative schools of Protestant theology, such as nineteenth-century German liberalism. The pertinent question, therefore, is, "Does evangelical diversity allow the presence of the open-theist?" Evangelicals "take it for granted that [they] are to give scripture the primary place and that everything else has to be lined up in relation to scripture."[13] The question is, does open theism—or more importantly, do open theists—line up? In other words, does ascription to open theology necessitate a non-evangelical understanding of Scripture?

Important to this discussion is the understanding that, while evangelicals believe that Scripture points the way to salvation, they do not believe that the affirmation of their understanding of Scripture is necessary for salvation. Take, for example, Article XIX of the 1978 Chicago Statement on Biblical Inerrancy:

> We affirm that a confession of the full authority, infallibility and inerrancy of Scripture is vital to a sound understanding of the whole of the Christian faith…We deny that such confession is necessary for salvation. However, we further deny that inerrancy can be rejected without grave consequences, both to the individual and to the Church.

Therefore, the issue at hand is the validity of an open theist's claim to the title "evangelical," not the legitimacy of his or her claim to the title "Christian."

The Authority of Scripture

A proper understanding of the evangelical concept of biblical authority is essential in understanding the evangelical mind. The Westminster Confession of Faith affirms that the

> authority of the Holy Scripture…depends not upon the testimony of any man, or Church; but wholly upon God (who is truth itself) the author thereof: and therefore it is to be received, because it is the Word of God.[14]

The preface to the 1978 Chicago Statement on Biblical Inerrancy argues that the "authority of Scripture is a key issue for the Christian Church in this and every age." It continues,

> Holy Scripture, being God's own Word, written by men prepared and superintended by His Spirit, is of infallible divine authority in all matters upon which it touches: It is to be believed, as God's instruction, in all that it affirms; obeyed, as God's command, in all that it requires; embraced, as God's pledge, in all that it promises (Summary 2).

Elsewhere, it expounds,

> As [Christ] bowed to His Father's instruction given in His Bible (our Old Testament), so He requires His disciples to do—not, however, in isolation but in conjunction with the apostolic witness to Himself that He undertook to inspire by His gift of the Holy Spirit. So Chris-

tians show themselves faithful servants of their Lord by bowing to the divine instruction given in the prophetic and apostolic writings that together make up our Bible (Exposition: Authority: Christ and the Bible).

Campus Crusade for Christ affirms that Scripture is the "supreme and final authority in all matters on which it speaks." The World Evangelical Alliance affirms Scripture as the "supreme authority of faith and conduct." Fuller Theological Seminary, in its doctrinal statement, "What We Believe and Teach," affirms this understanding of Scripture, stating that its own

> doctrinal commitment is built on a submission to the authority of Scripture, which must stand as teacher and judge of all that we think and do. It both inspires and corrects our doctrine and our conduct. It must always be clear that for us as Evangelicals, the Scriptures outrank all of our doctrinal statements, even statements as carefully written and as strongly believed as those in [this] Statement of Faith.

Evangelicals do not take the authority of Scripture lightly. To the evangelical mind, "what Scripture says, God says; its authority is His authority, for He is its ultimate Author."[15] Evangelicals everywhere agree that Scripture is authoritative in all matters of faith and practice.[16]

The key to understanding the place of open theology within evangelicalism, therefore, lies in ascertaining its compatibility with this understanding of Scripture. After all, according to evangelical belief, the "supreme judge by which all controversies of religion are to be determined…can be no other but the Holy Spirit speaking in the Scripture."[17] "For the evangelical, any theological stance which does not accept the inspiration and authority of Scripture cannot rightly call itself Orthodox."[18]

If the open theist can, without logical contradiction, affirm both open theology and these foundational evangelical beliefs, then he or she can rightfully claim the title "evangelical." If not, then the Evangelical Theological Society would have been justified in removing open theists from its membership roles.

Basics of Open Theology[19]

Since the publication of *The Openness of God* in 1994, open theology has become a hot topic of debate within evangelical circles. The controversy became so heated, in fact, that the Evangelical Theological Society brought to a vote a motion to remove Clark Pinnock and John Sanders from its membership rolls on account of their adherence to open theology.

While their membership was retained, the vote itself demonstrated the passion and fury open theology has inspired among evangelical scholars. In fact, in a taped interview, R. C. Sproul went so far as to question Pinnock's faith, stating, "Clark Pinnock is not a believer—I would not have fellowship with him."[20] More to the point, Paul R. House and Gregory A. Thornbury argue that "American Christianity is currently engaged in a crucial debate over the doctrine of God" and that "nothing less than the biblical, orthodox doctrines of God and of salvation are at stake."[21]

Open theology has arisen as a developed theological system in order to explain the revelation of God in Scripture that proponents feel traditional systematics have neglected.[22] At issue are passages testifying that God changes his mind, experiences regret and surprise, and hopes for a future that does not come to pass. Open theology also seeks to address philosophical issues, such as whether God foreknows free acts before they take place, and why God would create evil individuals, such as Adolf Hitler, despite knowing their future atrocities.[23]

While disagreements exist among open theists themselves, open theology takes the following basic form:

> God, in grace, grants humans significant freedom to cooperate with or work against God's will for their lives, and he enters into dynamic, give-and-take relationships with us. The Christian life involves a genuine interaction between God and human beings. We respond to God's gracious initiatives and God responds to our responses...and on it goes. God takes risks in this give-and-take relationship, yet he is endlessly resourceful and competent in working toward his ultimate goals. Sometimes God alone decides how to accomplish these goals. On other occasions, God works with human decisions, adapting his own plans to fit the changing situation. God does not control everything that happens. Rather, he is open to receiving input from his creatures. In loving dialogue, God invites us to participate with him to bring the future into being.[24]

There is an openness and interaction between God and man characteristic of genuine relationships. God and man work together to bring the future into existence in a give-and-take process of cooperation. Where other schools of thought may emphasize God's sovereignty or omnipotence, open theism—while not neglecting these divine attributes—stress relationship. In the open theist's mind, God can be understood only in terms of relationship. As I will discuss later, the open model of divine foreknowledge—the most controversial aspect of this belief system—reflects this emphasis.[25]

Open theists do not deny the omniscience of God. To say that open theology denies God's knowledge of the future, as opponents popularly frame openness, is to misunderstand—or misrepresent—the emphasis of this system of belief. Crass, pejorative comparisons to process theology do not do justice to the open position, but rather create a straw man to be torn down.[26]

A proper evaluation of the compatibility of open theology with evangelical understandings of Scripture requires a proper understanding of the beliefs open theists themselves claim as their own.

> The debate over the nature of God's foreknowledge is not primarily a debate about the scope or perfection of God's knowledge…[but] rather a debate over the *content of reality* that God perfectly knows. It has more to do with the doctrine of creation than it does with the doctrine of God.[27]

The traditional understanding of God's foreknowledge dictates that every event that has ever taken place or will ever take place in creation has existed as a settled metaphysical reality from all eternity. God, therefore, possesses knowledge of future events as certain as his knowledge of past events. Hence, any knowledge that God might have of possibility exists as "might have been, never as what might be."[28] All possibilities exist in God's knowledge in their exclusion from reality, rather than their inclusion therein. In other words, God knows all of reality as one eternally settled sequence of events.

Open theology, however, while maintaining God's omniscience, holds that the future consists of *both* certainties and possibilities and, consequently, some aspects of the future remain unsettled—that is, open—even to God.[29] God's omniscience, therefore, supplies God with knowledge of both settled events as settled and events that remain open as open.

Open theists believe that what aspects of the future are left open and what aspects are closed are determined by God. He is free to settle whatever aspects of the future he wants to settle, and upon doing so, brings certainty to those aspects of the future. Those aspects of the future God wills to leave open, however, remain uncertain, even to God.

Book Objective

This book's goal is to demonstrate the compatibility of open theology with the evangelical understandings of Scripture. Chapter 2 will evaluate passages of Scripture pertinent to the debate, both in favor of and in opposition to open theology. Since Scripture is of the utmost importance in the evangelical mind, the most time and energy will be devoted to this chapter.

Open theists frequently charge that opposition to their position in fact rests upon philosophical rather than scriptural grounds, and so Chapter 3 will evaluate the philosophical and systematic debate surrounding the open model of God within evangelical Christianity today. Chapter 3 will also touch on the practical implications open theology may have in the daily life of the believer. Finally, Chapter 4 will draw a conclusion to the question at hand, evaluating the coherence of the open model of God in relation to the evangelical label its adherents also claim.

This book does not seek to advocate the open model of God over and above any other theological school of thought. Rather, it seeks to establish open theism's place as a legitimate expression of evangelical theology. This requires a presentation of the interaction between open theism and other schools of thought, including the counterarguments open theists present against their opponents. This should not, however, be mistaken to mean that this book seeks to establish open theism as the most accurate expression of the biblical witness.

I hope that through this book, even those—like me—who are uncomfortable with open theism and reject its conclusions can garner some understanding of the open theist's position. In doing so, I hope that evangelicals can look past the shrill demagoguery of those seemingly incapable of distinguishing their understanding of sixteenth-century reformation theology from the actual message of Scripture, and, in doing so, can accept adherents of this school of thought as fellow believers and, indeed, as fellow evangelicals.

Endnotes

¹ For the purposes of this book, I use the term evangelical as it generally appears within modern Western culture and scholarship. The term has been applied in other parts of the world to all Christians who are not Roman Catholic and during the Reformation to distinguish the followers of Martin Luther from those of John Calvin (Richard Quebedeaux, *The Young Evangelicals: The Story of the Emergence of a New Generation of Evangelicals* (New York: Harper and Row, 1974), 3). All other uses of the term, as well as its association with neo-evangelicalism, are outside the scope of this book. Because of the nature of the debate, the word evangelical here and throughout this book refers to those holding to some form of *sola scriptura* and to the 66 book canon of the Protestant Bible and therefore excludes Roman Catholics claiming the title. Furthermore, it is important to note that the terms evangelical and fundamentalist are not synonymous. The fundamentalist movement is more narrow and hardline in its definition of the faith, leading a former President of Fuller Theological Seminary to label it "orthodoxy gone cultic" (Richard J. Moux, *The Smell of Sawdust: What Evangelicals Can Learn from Their Fundamentalist Heritage* (Grand Rapids: Zondervan, 2000), 39). Its positions are adequately defined in *The Fundamentals*, a series of essays compiled over several years in the early twentieth-century. Evangelicalism, among other things, allows for a historical-critical study of Scripture. (See generally the writings of George Ladd). Opposition to historical-critical study of Scripture is a central foundation to the fundamentalist movement. While the fundamentalist movement may have influenced modern evangelicalism, drastic differences between fundamentalist presuppositions and evangelical scholarly methodology makes the study of the fundamentalism unnecessary for the task at hand.

² Quebedeaux, 3-4.

³ J. I. Packer and Thomas C. Oden, *One Faith: The Evangelical Consensus* (Downers Grove, Illinois: InterVarsity Press, 2004), 21. Unless otherwise noted, all references throughout this chapter to the various evangelical statements of faith—except the Westminster Statement of Faith—are quoted as they appear in Packer and Oden, 39-57.

⁴ Where possible, I refer to evangelicals as holding to a "high view" of Scripture to avoid the intense emotional and academic baggage more exclusive terms, such as inerrancy and infallibility, carry. Debates regarding the proper terminology—with their complex nuances and varying implications—to associate with the evangelical view of Scripture are outside the scope of this book.

⁵ This book has no interest in proving the validity of either evangelical-

ism or open theism as they stand alone, only in determining their compatibility with one another.

⁶ N. T. Wright, "The Laing Lecture 1989 and the Griffith Thomas Lecture 1989," *Vox Evangelica* 21 (1991), available <http://www.ntwrightpage.com/Wright_Bible_Authoritative.htm> (19 September 2006).

⁷ Despite common ground among all evangelicals, there still exists disagreements over the nature of Scripture. Article XII of the Chicago Statement on Biblical Inerrancy, for example, affirms the scientific reliability of Scripture, denying that "scientific hypotheses about earth history may properly be used to overturn the teaching of Scripture on creation and the flood." This stands in opposition to the spirit of Fuller Theological Seminary's understanding of biblical inerrancy, which argues that applying the term inerrancy to "matters like chronological details, precise sequence of events, and numerical allusions," is "misleading and inappropriate" (Fuller Theological Seminary: What We Believe and Teach).

⁸ Quebedeaux, 4.

⁹ John H. Gerstner, "The Theological Boundaries of Evangelical Faith," in *The Evangelicals*, ed. David. F. Wells and John D. Woodbridge (Nashville: Abingdon Press, 1975), 23.

¹⁰ "Westminster Confession of Faith," available <http://www.reformed.org/documents/wcf_with_proofs/> (25 February 2007), ch. 1 sect. V.

¹¹ Quebedeaux, 4.

¹² "Amsterdam Declaration," 2000, Definitions, 4.

¹³ N. T. Wright, "Laing Lecture."

¹⁴ "The Westminster Confession of Faith," ch. 1 sect. IV.

¹⁵ "Chicago Statement on Biblical Inerrancy," 1978, Article IV.

¹⁶ Gerstner, 32.

¹⁷ "The Westminster Confession of Faith," ch. 1 sect X.

¹⁸ Quebedeaux, 5. "Orthodox" is capital in the original. Regardless, the source refers to right belief, making "orthodox" a more appropriate form. There is no reference to the Eastern Orthodox Church.

¹⁹ Except where otherwise noted, this section draws heavily from Greg Boyd's summary of open theology in "The Open-Theism View," in *Divine Foreknowledge: Four Views*, ed. James K. Beilby and Paul R. Eddy (Downers Grove, Illinois: InterVarsity Press, 2001): 13-47.

²⁰ Clark H. Pinnock, *Most Moved Mover* (Grand Rapids: Baker Academic, 2001), 16.

²¹ P. R. House and G. A. Thornbury (eds.), *Who Will Be Saved? Defending the Biblical Understanding of God, Salvation, and Evangelism* (Wheaton: Crossway Books, 2000), 15, quoted in Pinnock, *Most Moved Mover*, 17.

22 Here and throughout this book, the term traditional refers to those holding to the commonly accepted understanding of divine foreknowledge over and against the position of open theism. These theologians are commonly referred to as classical theologians by open theists. Augustine, Aquinas, and Calvin are major proponents of this sort of theological understanding. While there could be a technical distinction between classical and traditional theologies, the two terms are used interchangeably throughout this book.

23 Gregory A. Boyd, *God of the Possible* (Grand Rapids: Baker Books, 2000), 10.

24 Clark Pinnock and others, *The Openness of God* (Downers Grove: InterVarsity Press, 1994), 7.

25 Because of their association with other theological debates, a definition of terms is in order. Foreknowledge is a term generally associated with Arminianism. Foreknowledge in this sense is God's ability to peer into the future and foreknow what will transpire, even if he will have no direct involvement in the event. Predestination, however, is a term generally associated with Calvinism. God knows what the future holds because he has predestined it. In other words, in Arminianism, God's knowledge of future events is based on the future. In Calvinism, future events are based on the foreknowledge (predestination) of God. Unless otherwise noted, throughout this book, the term foreknowledge refers to God's knowledge of future events, whether that be through the Arminian understanding of foreknowledge or the Calvinistic understanding of predestination.

26 Process theology is a liberal theological movement holding, among other things, that God's existence depends on the existence of creation and that God's power is limited by forces outside his own will. For a critique of process theology from an evangelical position, see R. Nash, ed., *Process Theology* (Grand Rapids: Baker, 1987) (Boyd, *God of the Possible*, 170). Process theology holds that God cannot predestine or foreknow any aspect of the distant future with any kind of certainty, while open theology maintains God's ability to determine and foreknow whatever he wants about future events. Proponents of open theology maintain that, while God could certainly micromanage everything about creation and determine all future events, he has chosen not to do so. The open nature of some aspects of the future, according to open theists, is a result of God's free choice to leave aspects of the future to be determined by the free will of others (Boyd, *God of the Possible*, 31). To compare open theology and process theology as related theological positions, therefore, is unwarranted and counterproductive for healthy scholarly debate.

27 Boyd, "The Open-Theism View," 13.

28 Ibid.

[29] Ibid., 14.

2 SCRIPTURE

No issue is more central to the debate surrounding the place of open theists within evangelicalism than the compatibility of open theism with Scripture. While issues of philosophy and systematics are important when determining a theology's validity, the implications of *sola scriptura* allow any theological position to gain at least reluctant toleration within evangelicalism if it proves to be consistent with a reasonable interpretation of the biblical witness.[1]

Questioning Exhaustive Divine Foreknowledge

Divine Repentance

No single biblical motif plays a more central role in the battle between open and classical theology than that of divine repentance. How a God with exhaustive foreknowledge of future events can actually change his mind is logically problematic. Open theists use divine repentance to build a biblical case for their position, while traditionalists try to reconcile the biblical witness with their own theological understandings of the divine nature.

Before the biblical validity of open theism can be ascertained, however, the legitimacy of its argument for divine repentance must be evaluated through a careful analysis of biblical texts addressing the matter. What follows is a careful walkthrough of scriptural passages that directly speak to this controversial subject.

(i) Exodus 32:7-14

Of all the passages of Scripture speaking to the issue of divine repentance, few garner as much attention as Exodus 32, where, in dramatic fashion, Moses successfully convinces Yahweh to refrain from destroying the Israelites. Because of its centrality within the controversy surrounding the issue, I will spend the most time on this passage, allowing my exegetical analysis of its teachings to lay the foundation for later discussion on the topic.

> Then Yahweh said to Moses, "Go down, because your people, whom you brought up out of Egypt, have become corrupt. They have been quick to turn away from what I commanded them and have made themselves an idol cast in the shape of a calf. They have bowed down to it and sacrificed to it and have said, 'These are your gods, O Israel, who brought you up out of Egypt.' I have seen these people," Yahweh said to Moses, "and they are stiff-necked people. Now leave me alone so that my anger may burn against them and that I may destroy them. Then I will make you into a great nation (Exodus 32:7-10).[2]

The heart of the story lies in the contrast between the apostasy occurring in the valley and the giving of the covenant on the mountain. Verse 7 marks an immediate shift from the scene of merrymaking in the Israelite camp as they celebrate in the shadow of their new idol (v. 6) to Yahweh's immediate reaction (vv. 7-10).[3]

A "momentum of haste" builds in the narrative as Yahweh creates an urgency through his quick, successive use of verbs: "Go down!...you brought up...have become corrupt...have been quick to turn away...have made themselves an idol...have bowed down to it and have sacrificed to it...have said...." These are intermeshed with verbs referencing Yahweh himself: "I commanded...I have seen...my anger may burn...I may destroy...I will make you...."[4]

Yahweh, in the midst of making his covenant with Israel, quickly changes his attitude in response to her quick apostasy, as if to say, "[t]here is no purpose in continuing with covenant laws when the covenant has been shattered."[5] Earlier, Yahweh had referred to the Israelites as "my people" and "my firstborn son" (4:22). No longer. They now belong to Moses.[6] Yahweh's fury at the infidelity of the people culminates in his disowning them.[7] From the beginning, the covenant has been conditioned upon the obedience of the Israelites. Now that they have broken it, Yahweh declares the covenant null and void.[8]

Israel has corrupted herself (v.7), condemning herself with her own words: "These are your gods."[9] The ramifications of Israel's fateful decision would echo throughout her history, as the rabbis themselves counted the golden calf incident the worst sin of Israel's entire history, going so far as to declare, "Had Israel waited for Moses and not perpetrated that act, there would have been no exile, neither would the Angel of Death have had any power over them."[10]

Yahweh's contempt surfaces in his derogatory reference to the Israelites as "these people" (v. 9) and his crediting Moses with the Exodus (v. 7), a clear parody of the Israelites' disparaging reference to Moses as "this fellow,"[11] and their crediting Moses with the Exodus event in verse 1.

> In effect, God informs Moses that if this is what the people want to believe and confess, let them. But…if they wish to make confession of a deliverer other than Yahweh, then they will have to bear the consequences.[12]

Here the openness argument finds validation. This passage demonstrates Yahweh's reaction to the people's behavior. It does not describe the impassible God of classical philosophical thought, knowing from eternity the inevitability of this sin. Rather, it depicts Yahweh as a vulnerable God, reacting in pain to the rejection he has experienced at the hands of his people. The text suggests that Yahweh is genuinely wounded by the people's rejection.[13]

After an emotional outburst, Yahweh reaches a fateful decision, which demonstrates his willingness—and ability—to change his plans radically in response to the deeds of his people. He declares his intentions to completely annihilate the Israelites, throwing the nation's special election into the balance.[14]

The narrative leaves no room for ambiguity regarding Yahweh's rage. The whole of the Exodus account thus far has followed Yahweh's fulfillment of his promise to the patriarchs. By transferring his promise from Abraham to Moses, and thereby setting Moses up as a new Abraham, Yahweh demonstrates just how serious he is about wiping out the Israelites and starting over his plans to bless Abraham's descendants with Moses.[15] The text does not substantiate the argument that Yahweh is simply putting on a show to teach Moses a lesson. Every indication is that Yahweh is serious about carrying out his proposal.

In the verses that follow, open theology gains one of its most powerful points in arguing its case. In his reaction of anger, Yahweh reveals another side of himself. The Hebrew word translated here, "leave me alone," is one of the most explicit words in all of Scripture emphasizing Yahweh's vulnerability.[16] The root word means "to let something lie in a place, to leave behind, to let something remain, to allow something to happen, or, in five occurrences, all in the imperative, to let someone alone."[17]

For example, in 2 Samuel 16:11, David tells those who want to kill Shimei for cursing him to *"leave him alone*; let him curse" (emphasis added), and in Hosea 4:16-17, Yahweh says through Hosea, "The Israelites are stubborn, like a stubborn heifer. How then can Yahweh pasture them like lambs in a meadow? Ephraim is joined to idols; *leave him alone!*" (emphasis added). In each of these passages, someone with power over another is asked to refrain. Only once in the entire Bible is Yahweh the one affected by the request, as the omnipotent God asks a human being to "leave me alone so that..."[18] demonstrating a relational aspect of Yahweh's character.

Now, for this phrase to make sense, Yahweh must already have decided to judge the Israelites;[19] yet for some reason, he surrenders some of his power to Moses. He is simply unwilling to act without drawing Moses into the decision-making process.[20]

Yahweh could very well shut the door on any possibility of intercession, as he does in Deuteronomy 3:26 when Moses pleads with Yahweh to allow him to enter the Promised Land.[21] Here, however, Yahweh threatens the worst possible punishment but conditions it upon Moses' willingness to leave him alone. "Moses could conceivably contribute something to the divine deliberation that might occasion a future for Israel other than wrath."[22]

A tension builds as the reader expects Moses now to attempt to "calm Yahweh."[23]

> But Moses sought the favor of Yahweh his God, "O Yahweh," he said, "why should your anger burn against your people, whom you brought out of Egypt with great power and a mighty hand? Why should the Egyptians say, 'It was with evil intent that he brought them out, to kill them in the mountains and to wipe them off the face of the earth'? Turn from your fierce anger: relent and do not bring disaster on your people. Remember your servants Abraham, Isaac and Israel, to whom you swore by your own self: 'I will make your descendants as numerous as the stars in the sky and I will give your descendants all this land I promised them, and it will be their inheritance forever.'" Then Yahweh relented and did not bring on his people the disaster he had threatened (vv. 11-14).

Moses refuses to concede to Yahweh's request.[24] Instead of accepting Yahweh's intentions, he pleads for the people,[25] whose interests he has learned to put first. Moses begins to reason with Yahweh,[26] trying to persuade him from doing what he has threatened.[27] He shifts Yahweh's language, reaffirming that the Israelites are indeed "your people, whom you brought out of Egypt" (v. 11).

Moses then begins to make a series of arguments in his effort to persuade Yahweh. First, Yahweh had hitherto gone to great lengths to ensure the people's deliverance from Egypt.[28] Not only did the Israelites not want to leave Egypt in the first place, but as soon as they got into the wilderness, they wanted to turn back. Yahweh had to go to even greater lengths to convince Pharaoh to let the Israelites go, and the plagues of Egypt and the deliverance through the Red Sea demonstrate that the universe itself had to be disrupted in order to deliver the Israelites.[29]

Of course, the golden calf incident is much worse than the previous "murmuring in the wilderness," but does that justify total annihilation of the people? Moses is asking Yahweh to be reasonable![30] He has already brought them too far to destroy them in the wilderness.[31] If he were to follow through with his plan, the entire Exodus event would be for naught.[32]

Second, the Egyptians will misunderstand Yahweh's actions, not as a fair and just judgment for sin, but as a display of Yahweh's evil intentions.[33] A recurring theme throughout the Exodus narrative (as well as throughout the prophets) is Yahweh's acting in such a way that Egypt and all the nations may know that he is God.[34] Moses puts Yahweh's very honor at stake.[35]

Third, Yahweh should have mercy on the Israelites—who are, after all, his own people—in the face of such disaster befalling them. Lastly, Moses invokes the Abrahamic covenant, reminding Yahweh of the oath he made with the Israelites' forefathers to make their descendants numerous and bring them into a great land.[36] Yahweh "has made a commitment to Israel, and would not God be following the same course as the people by going back on such a promise?"[37]

Of course, these are not arguments that Yahweh has yet to consider. Indeed, his promise to make Moses into a great nation shows that he had his promise to Abraham in mind. The advocate, and not the arguments themselves, makes the difference. Yahweh is open to hear from Moses, whose opinions form a central ingredient in Yahweh's formation of future events.[38]

> If Moses wills and thinks and does these things, they take on a significance that they do not carry when treated in divine isolation. It is not a matter of Moses' winning the argument but of a relationship that God takes seriously.[39]

Moses pleads with Yahweh to "relent" (v. 12), sometimes translated "repent."[40] This same Hebrew word appears in Genesis 6:7, when Yahweh describes his intentions to destroy mankind: "Yahweh said, 'I will blot out man whom I have created from the face of the land, from man to animals to creeping things and to birds of the sky; for *I am sorry* that I have made them" (NASB, emphasis added). In Deuteronomy 32:26 the same word appears again: "Yahweh will judge his people and *have compassion* on his servants" (emphasis added). In addition, Judges 2:18 reads,

> Whenever Yahweh raised up a judge for them, he was with the judge and saved them out of the hands of their enemies as long as the judge lived; for Yahweh *had compassion* on them as they groaned under those who oppressed and afflicted them (emphasis added).

The word expresses a change of heart. Here, Moses urges Yahweh to repent from his intended wrath and have compassion on the Israelites instead.

When Moses finishes his argument, Yahweh is silent. Yet the text makes it clear that Moses has moved him to pity Israel for his own threats against her,[41] stating only that "Yahweh relented."[42]

While the text does imply that Yahweh's anger is tempered, it does not say he totally withdraws his judgment. Exodus 32-34 gives an account of Yahweh's severe—though significantly reduced—punishment.[43] Yahweh is "merciful and gracious...but will not clear the guilty."[44] Nevertheless, this passage demonstrates a change of heart on Yahweh's part, contributing greatly to the scriptural motif of divine repentance and the resulting ramifications for systematic theology.

A brief survey of the Pentateuch, however, demonstrates that Moses' intervention and Yahweh's repentance do not change this generation's eventual fate. They all do eventually die in the wilderness as a result of God's judgment, save Joshua and Caleb. This does not, however, negate Yahweh's change of heart or the biblical motif of divine repentance. Yahweh never directly destroys the nation as he threatens in this passage; he simply waits until the current generation dies off before leading Israel into Canaan.

Nevertheless, in a very real way, Moses' intervention saves the lives of future generations of Israelites. Yahweh does, after all, show mercy to all those Israelites under twenty years old at the time the people refused to go up and take the Promised Land, an act of mercy never suggested in Exodus 32. Yahweh's repentance in this passage delays judgment, giving the people more opportunities to mend their ways. Their refusal to do so does not prove Yahweh's repentance in this chapter insincere. Indeed, why would Yahweh have delayed judgment if he knew with absolute certainty that judgment was inevitable?[45]

This passage, with its descriptions of Yahweh's threat to destroy his people and his subsequent repentance, is difficult to reconcile with the doctrine of exhaustive divine foreknowledge. At least in this passage, the open model of a God in dynamic relationship with human beings facing a future that is to some extent uncertain adheres nicely to the biblical witness. In fact, open theists have a much easier time making sense of this passage—and those like it—than do those holding to a traditional understanding of divine foreknowledge.

(ii) Jeremiah 18:7-10

Where Exodus 32 provides a narrative account of Yahweh's changing his mind, Jeremiah 18 provides Yahweh's personal affirmation of his ability to do so. Through his prophet, Yahweh addresses the people's belief that his judgment has been promised and so there is no use in repenting.

> Now therefore say to the people of Judah and those living in Jerusalem, "This is what Yahweh says: 'Look! I am preparing a disaster for you and devising a plan against you. So turn from your evil ways, each one of you, and reform your ways and your actions.' But they will reply, 'It's no use. We will continue with our own plans; each of us will follow the stubbornness of his evil heart'" (18:11-12).

However, Yahweh quickly corrects this mistaken belief that "It's no use" to repent.

> At one moment I may declare concerning a nation or a kingdom, that I will pluck up and break down and destroy it, but if that nation, concerning which I have spoken, turns from its evil, I will *change my mind* about the disaster that I intended to bring on it. And at another moment I may declare concerning a nation or kingdom that I will build and plant it, but if it does evil in my sight, not listening to my voice, then I will *change my mind* about the good that I had intended to do to it (vv. 7-10, NRSV, emphasis added).

Not only does the scriptural narrative describe Yahweh's changing his mind as historical fact, but through his prophet, Yahweh actually *promises* to do so if his people will only repent. The classical argument that God cannot change his mind runs into a serious obstacle in this passage. Many may claim that divine repentance is merely phenomenological, but if God cannot change his mind, how can Jeremiah 18:7-10 be anything other than a divine deception?

(iii) The Book of Jonah

The prophetic promise of Jeremiah 18 finds its narrative fulfillment in the book of Jonah. Here, Yahweh makes what seems to be an unconditional promise that he will destroy Nineveh within forty days. Upon hearing Jonah's message, however, the people humble themselves and repent. "When God saw what they did and how they turned from their evil ways, he had compassion and did not bring upon them the destruction he had threatened" (3:10).[46]

Jonah knew withholding judgment in response to repentance to be characteristic of the divine nature. So seriously did Jonah take Yahweh's ability to change his mind that he actually ran away from his assigned task of preaching in Nineveh in order to prevent their being shown mercy. "I knew that you are a gracious and compassionate God, slow to anger and abounding in love, a God who *relents* [literally, repents] from sending calamity" (4:2b).[47]

Clement of Rome[48] points to this event in Scripture as an example of divine mercy, declaring it to be a manifestation of the very character of God. "Jonah foretold destruction to the men of Nineveh, but when they repented they received forgiveness of their sins from God in answer to their prayer, and gained salvation, though they were aliens to God" (1 Clement 7:7).

Attempts to explain away this entire book of Scripture in order to maintain the impossibility of genuine divine repentance rob Jonah of its message. God's character is such that mercy overrules judgment. If he declares judgment and in response the people repent, he too will repent.

Indeed, is not God's granting forgiveness an example of divine repentance? If he holds a person in a place of judgment but then in response to repentance extents grace, has he not himself repented of his intended judgment with regard to that person?[49] Scripture suggests that people have a choice between two ways: a way of obedience and a way of disobedience. God has already determined how he will deal with people based on which path they choose.

God's ability to change his mind, however, suggests that which of these two ways a person will choose is as open ended from the divine perspective as it is from the anthropological. If a sinner will repent, God will repent as well.

> The ministers of the grace of God spoke through the Holy Spirit concerning repentance, and even the Master of the universe himself spoke with an oath concerning repentance; "For as I live, said the Lord, I do not desire the death of the sinner so much as his repentance," and he added a gracious declaration, "Repent, O house of Is-

rael, from your iniquity. Say to the sons of my people, If your sins reach from the dearth to Heaven, and if they be redder than scarlet, and blacker than sackcloth, and ye turn to me with all your hearts and say 'Father,' I will listen to you as a holy people" (1 Clement 8:1-3).

(iv) Other passages

The vast number of passages testifying to the reality of divine repentance makes a full analysis of each instance impossible within the confines of this book. For the purpose at hand, a brief look at a few other passages supporting the open position of divine repentance will suffice.

Multiple other passages throughout the Scripture gives credence to the view that God does in fact change his mind. In fact, the Old Testament affirms God's ability to change his mind twenty-four different times.[50] For example, in 1 Chronicles 21:15, Yahweh sends an angel to destroy Jerusalem but becomes distressed at the sight of the destruction and rescinds his order.

In 2 Kings 20, Yahweh declares through Isaiah that King Hezekiah will soon die from his illness. Hezekiah, however, weeps and prays to Yahweh, "Remember, O Yahweh, how I have walked before you faithfully and with wholehearted devotion and have done what is good in your eyes" (2 Kings 20:3). Yahweh responds, "I have heard your prayer and seen your tears; I will heal you. On the third day from now you will go up to the temple of Yahweh. I will add fifteen years to your life" (vv. 5-6).

Other examples include Exodus 33:1-3, in which Yahweh says to Moses,

> Leave this place, you and the people you brought up out of Egypt, and go up to the land I promised on oath to Abraham, Isaac and Jacob, saying, "I will give it to your descendants." I will send an angel before you and drive out the Canaanites, Amorites, Hittites, Perizzites, Hivites and Jebusites. Go up to the land flowing with milk and honey. But I will not go with you, because you are a stiff-necked people and I might destroy you on the way.[51]

Moses responds,

> You have been telling me, "Lead these people," but you have not let me know whom you will send with me. You have said, "I know you by name and you have found favor with me." If you are pleased with me, teach me your ways so I may know you and continue to find favor with you. Remember that this nation is your people (vv. 12-13).

In response to Moses' plea, Yahweh reverses his position, stating simply, "My Presence will go with you, and I will give you rest" (v. 14). After further discussion, Yahweh gives the reason for this reversal. "I will do the very thing you have asked, because I am pleased with you and I know you by name" (v. 17). Here, Yahweh makes explicit what is implicit throughout Scripture: he is willing to change his mind and adjust his plans in response to the pleas and requests of his people. Indeed, the story of Scripture is the story of a God who not only influences but allows himself to be influenced. Consider also Jeremiah 26:18-19.

> Micah of Moresheth prophesied in the days of Hezekiah king of Judah. He told all the people of Judah, "This is what Yahweh Almighty says: 'Zion will be plowed like a field, Jerusalem will become a heap of rubble, the temple hill a mound overgrown with thickets.'" Did Hezekiah king of Judah or anyone else in Judah put him to death? Did not Hezekiah fear Yahweh and seek his favor? And did not Yahweh *relent*, so that he did not bring the disaster he pronounced against them? We are about to bring a terrible disaster on ourselves! (emphasis added).

Clearly Yahweh is trying to present himself to the people as a God who will change his mind. He promises to repent of the wrath he has planned for them if they will repent of their sins (cf. Jer 18:7-10), and the text reinforces the validity of that promise by pointing to a past example of his actually having done so.[52]

Other key passages include Deuteronomy 9:13-29—in which Moses convinces Yahweh to abandon his plans to destroy the Israelites—1 Samuel 2:27-36—in which the sins of Eli's son cause Yahweh to retract his promise that Eli's house would maintain the priestly line forever—and 1 Kings 21:21-29—in which Ahab's demonstration of humility prompts Yahweh to delay his promised judgment of Ahab's house.

Other important passages include 2 Chronicles 12:5-8, Jeremiah 26:2-3, Ezekiel 4:9-15, Amos 7:1-6, Numbers 11:1-2, Numbers 14:12-20, Numbers 16:20-35, Numbers 16:41-48, Judges 10:13-16, 2 Samuel 24:17-25, 2 Kings 13:3-5, 2 Chronicles 7:12-14, Jeremiah 7:5-7, Ezekiel 33:13-15, and Hosea 11:8-9. These passages either explicitly state that God has or will change his mind in response to his people. The sheer number of these passages demands attention. Ironically, open theists have been accused of failing to hold a high view of Scripture precisely because they take such passages seriously.

Building on the theme of divine repentance, I now will explore a variety of related scriptural motifs regarding the divine character. I borrow these motifs from Terence Fretheim's *Suffering of God*, and except where otherwise stated, what follows in the next few pages is a general overview of his compelling work.

The Divine Perhaps[53]

The Hebrew word frequently translated "perhaps" appears in divine speech five times in the Old Testament. The two passages most pertinent to this discussion are Ezekiel 12:1-3 and Jeremiah 26:2-3.

> The word of Yahweh came to me: "Son of man, you are living among a rebellious people. They have eyes to see but do not see and ears to hear but do not hear, for they are a rebellious people. Therefore, son of man, pack your belongings for exile and in the daytime, as they watch, set out and go from where you are to another place. *Perhaps* they will understand, though they are a rebellious house (Ezek 12:1-3; emphasis added).

> This is what Yahweh says: Stand in the courtyard of Yahweh's house and speak to all people of the towns of Judah who come to worship in the house of Yahweh. Tell them everything I command you; do not omit a word. *Perhaps* they will listen and each will turn from his evil way. Then I will relent and not bring on them the disaster I was planning because of the evil they had done (Jer 26:2-3; emphasis added).

These passages seem to indicate that, while Yahweh is certainly aware of Israel's various possible responses, he is "quiet uncertain as to how the people will respond to the prophetic word."[54] While the texts never suggest that the future will take Yahweh by complete surprise, Yahweh's own words indicate that there is still a lack of definite certainty regarding future events, even in his own mind.

> Every indication in these texts would suggest that God, knowing the depths of Israel's sin, should have been able to declare unequivocally that judgment was inevitable. This God does not do; it is possible that some spontaneous response to the preaching of the prophets will pull them out of the fire at the last moment. Thus, we can say generally that even if God knows every causal factor involved in shaping Israel's future, God still recognizes all this knowledge as being an insufficient basis for predicting that future in detail. For the future is not entirely shaped by such causes; there is room for spontaneity. And God in essence is hoping that an unpredictable event might, in fact, occur.[55]

This line of reasoning drives a major aspect of open theology. If Yahweh knew with absolute certainty that Israel would not repent, then his statement to Ezekiel that "perhaps they will understand" and his statement to Jeremiah that "perhaps they will listen" are simply deceptive.[56] Jeremiah 3, with its presentation of divine uncertainty, further drives this line of thinking.

> "I thought that after she had done all this she would return to me but she did not, and her unfaithful sister Judah has no fear; she also went out and committed adultery…'How gladly would I treat you like sons and give you a desirable land, the most beautiful inheritance of any nation.' I thought you would call me 'Father' and not turn away from following me. But like a woman unfaithful to her husband, so you have been unfaithful to me, O house of Israel," declares Yahweh (vv. 8, 19).

God actually confesses to having had an overly optimistic outlook of the future. The people simply did not react as he thought they would, strongly suggesting that God possesses only a limited knowledge of future human actions—because they do not yet exist to be known.

What is at stake here, tied in with an understanding of God's foreknowledge, is God's integrity in his command to his prophets. If God knew with absolutely certainty how Israel would respond, then God's words are deceptive.

Some may suggest that perhaps, for some unknown reason, God had to describe the situation this way despite actually knowing Israel's response with certainty. This, however, sacrifices the integrity and coherence of the divine word in order to preserve a theological presupposition. Furthermore, there is simply no textual justification for this strained reading. Rather, the texts argue that Israel's future is open and has not been finally determined. Therefore, her future cannot be known, even by God himself.

Fretheim describes the situation well when he writes,

> It may be said that God knows God's ultimate salvific goals for the people and world will be achieved one way or another, and that God's purposes in moving toward those goals will be constant. But there are innumerable paths for the people to take along the way; these are known to God as probabilities or possibilities. A limited analogy may help: when I play chess with my young daughter, I know the possibility for play which she has, how I will respond to them, and that I will finally win the game….The way in which the game will progress and finally be won, and the amount of time it will take, however, will be determined only in light of the various moves

she will make.[57]

In these instances, God and Israel are both presented as having somewhat open-ended futures with Israel's actions playing a role not only in determining her own future, but also God's. In other words, "what God will do at least in part depends on what Israel does."[58]

The Divine If

Running parallel to the "perhaps" passages of divine speech are conditional statements. For example, Jeremiah 7:5-7 reads,

> *If* you really change your ways and your actions and deal with each other justly, *if* you do not oppress the alien, the fatherless or the widow and do not shed innocent blood in this place, and *if* you do not follow other gods to your own harm, *then* I will let you live in this place, in the land I gave your forefathers for ever and ever (emphasis added).

The people's staying in the land is conditioned upon their repentance. God's future action must be a possibility, not a certainty, if there is to be any integrity to his promise. If God knew with certainty at the moment he delivered this oracle that the people would not repent and would therefore not stay in the land, then he is deceiving the people, holding out a false hope.

Jeremiah 22:4-5 likewise presents both negative and positive possibilities for the future.

> "For *if* you are careful to carry out these commands, *then* kings who sit on David's throne will come through the gates of this place, riding in chariots and on horses, accompanied by their officials and their people. But *if* you do not obey these commands," declares Yahweh, "I swear by myself that this palace will come to ruin" (emphasis added).

Which possible future comes to pass is dependent on the king's willingness to heed Yahweh's calls for justice. Each of these options has integrity only if God does not know with absolutely certainly which possibility will come to pass. In order for it to be a "genuine possibility for the king, then it must be a possibility, and only a possibility, for God as well."[59]

To open theists, God is able to grasp every possible future and its likelihood of occurrence in light of his full and complete knowledge of past and present realities, but the future is a realm of possibilities, which thereby limits his ability to know with certainty which of these possible futures will actually come to pass. To them, a complete certainty of all future events as fixed and inalterable realities simply does not square with the Old Testament's view of omniscience.[60] And nowhere does the Old Testament suggest this limits God's knowledge or power.

Consider also Exodus 4, in which Moses asks Yahweh what will happen if the Israelite elders don't believe him, as Yahweh promised they would in 3:18. Yahweh does not respond, "I told you they would believe you, so they will." Instead, he offers Moses a miracle as a means of persuasion (4:5).

Moses is still skeptical, so Yahweh performs a second miracle saying, "*If* they do not believe you or pay attention to the first miraculous sign, they *may* believe the second" (4:8; emphasis added). Yahweh then adds, "But *if* they do not believe these two signs or listen to you, take some water from the Nile and pour it on the dry ground. The water you take from the river will become blood on the ground" (v. 9; emphasis added).

If Yahweh possessed definite foreknowledge of the elders' response, he would have known exactly how many miracles would have been necessary to sway them. For Yahweh to be sincere in this conversation, however, he too must lack the certainty to say definitively how many miracles would be necessary. This passage "demonstrates that God is perfectly confident in his ability to achieve the results he is looking for (getting the elders of Israel to listen to Moses) even though he works with free agents who are, to some extent, unpredictable."[61]

In Exodus 3:17, Yahweh decides to guide Israel to the promised land on a longer path so as to avoid encountering the Philistines because he thinks "*If* they face war, they *might* change their minds and return to Egypt" (emphasis added). Boyd argues that if "we accept this language as inspired by God, doesn't it clearly imply that God considered the *possibility*, but not the *certainty*, that the Israelites would change their minds if they faced battle?"[62]

These passages demonstrate a view of divine foreknowledge unpopular in evangelical circles, for they show God's facing the future without absolute certainty as to the events that shall transpire. Though open theists adamantly affirm that God is omniscient, they contend that only so much of the future exists to be known, precluding exhaustive foreknowledge of future events, even for God.

"Since God is omniscient and knows reality exactly as it is, these passages suggest that the future consists in part of things that might or might not happen."[63] Therefore, open theists do, in fact, argue that God knows the future. The future, however, exists in terms of possibilities, not certainties, and consequently God, whose knowledge encompasses all of reality as it truly is, knows it as such.

The Divine Consultation

Throughout the Old Testament, God demonstrates his willingness and readiness to take human thought and action into consideration when making decisions. This biblical motif is demonstrated in God's repetitive consultations with prophetic leaders. Consider Genesis 18.

> Then Yahweh said, "Shall I hide from Abraham what I am about to do? Abraham will surely become a great and powerful nation, and all nations on earth will be blessed through him. For I have chosen him, so that he will direct his children and his household after him to keep the way of Yahweh by doing what is right and just, so that Yahweh will bring about for Abraham what he has promised him" (vv. 17-19).

Before Yahweh follows through on his plans of judgment against Sodom and Gomorrah, he reveals them to Abraham, involving him in the divine decision. The text implies that, given the nature of the relationship between Yahweh and Abraham, Yahweh's exclusion of Abraham from the decision-making process would be unnatural.

Yet again, for the ensuing conversation between Yahweh and Abraham to have any integrity, Yahweh's judgment of Sodom must only be a possibility—albeit a likely one—and not a certainty. Yahweh is clearly waiting on the outcome of his consultation with Abraham before he makes the final decision, demonstrating once again that God takes human thought into consideration when shaping the future. Even if Yahweh has already decided to destroy Sodom and Gomorrah, however, and this dialogue with Abraham is more about bringing Abraham into relationship with Yahweh, this passage still demonstrates a dynamic understanding of divine-human relations so heavily emphasized by open theology.

Consider also Amos 7:1-6.

> This is what the Sovereign LORD showed me: He was preparing swarms of locusts after the king's share had been harvested and just as the second crop was coming up. When they had stripped the land clean, I cried out, "Sovereign LORD, forgive! How can Jacob survive? He is so small!" So the LORD relented. "This will not happen," the LORD said. This is what the Sovereign LORD showed me: The Sovereign LORD was calling for judgment by fire; it dried up the great deep and devoured the land. Then I cried out, "Sovereign LORD, I beg you, stop! How can Jacob survive? He is so small!" So the LORD relented. "This will not happen either," the Sovereign LORD said.

This passage demonstrate that Yahweh's decision for Israel's future is not irrevocably certain. Yahweh gives Amos the opportunity to respond, and twice he is successful in turning away God's wrath. "The initial announcement of God's decision of judgment means that that is a probable future for Israel, but the openness to Amos's response entailed in the announcement means that there is also another possibility for the future which is just as real for God as for Israel."[64]

Consider also Amos 3:7. "Surely the Sovereign LORD does nothing without revealing his plan to his servants the prophets." The above excerpt from Amos 7 demonstrates that this does not mean Yahweh only announces determined future certainties to his prophets, but rather that he draws them into the sphere of divine decision-making regarding future events. The future remains open, waiting for the results yielded by the prophetic conversation.

Amos 7:1-6 demonstrates that the "announcement of God to the prophets does not have the status of an immutable decree, but of a possibility to be explored together..."[65] Yahweh's ordering Jeremiah to cease his intercession further demonstrates this point (Jer 7:16; 11:14; 14:11). The prohibition of intercession reveals that the realm of possible futures has been reduced to one: judgment.

From these passages comes a clearer understanding of the divine-human relationship. God's plan for the world should not be envisioned as some overarching, idealistic destiny, unalterable and impersonal, like fate. Rather, human beings are participants in the divine design, working with God to craft an uncertain future into being.

> Abraham Heschel, the great Jewish student of the Prophets, underscores [the prophets'] spirit of protest. "The refusal to accept the harshness of God's ways in the name of his love was an authentic form of prayer. Indeed, the ancient Prophets of Israel were not in the habit of consenting to God's harsh judgment and did not simply nod, saying 'Thy will be done.' They often challenged him, as if to say, 'Thy will be changed.'" Henscehl adds, "Man should never capitulate, even to the Lord."[66]

The Divine Question

Certain divine questions recorded in the Old Testament further support the openness position.

> What can I do with you, Ephraim? What can I do with you, Judah? (Hosea 6:4).

Why should I forgive you? Your children have forsaken me and sworn by gods that are not gods...Should I not punish them for this? (Jer 5:7, 9).

These divine questions run parallel to the divine consultation motif. God interrupts announcements of judgment to ask these questions in order to elicit repentance from the people. "When God shares such questions with Israel about its own future, God's questions then become questions for Israel, and they are drawn into the process of moving toward an answer."[67]

The people's response answers the question. Should they repent, the tension is resolved. Should they refuse, however, the question is answered with judgment. In the divine consultation motif, God shares the divine decision-making process with prophetic leaders. Through these divine questions God extends that privilege to all the people. The point of these questions is to make clear that the decision for judgment is not irrevocable but is rather open-ended, to be determined by the people's response. Implicit through this is the understanding that the future will bring new knowledge, not only for the people, but for God as well.

This is not an example of God's indecisiveness. He has already made the decision. God, however, remains open to the possibility of changing his mind. He is willing to consult with the people and take their response into consideration before finalizing his decision and following through.

God holds back on a final decision, not because God is indecisive, but because God wants the decision to be shared. And yet, it is a genuine question for God, and one from which God will learn, as God and people move toward an answer together.[68]

All of these biblical motifs, from divine repentance to the divine question, suggest a genuine openness to the future that even God must face because he chose to order reality the way that he has. An Old Testament understanding of divine omniscience regarding the future must be limited to the parameters Scripture itself sets. Open theology therefore finds an immense amount of support for its position in the biblical witness. In fact, very often it is the most natural way to understand the implications of the text.

Some may argue that the major support for the open model of God lies in the Old Testament, thus undermining its validity. This, however, contradicts evangelical understandings of revelation. As Article V of the 1978 Chicago Statement on Biblical Inerrancy states, "We deny that later revelation, which may fulfill earlier revelation, ever corrects or contradicts it."

If the God of the Old Testament faces on open future, then the God of the New Testament does as well. Furthermore, the almost total lack of explicit and apparent divine action in New Testament narrative—save of course, Christ's—leaves the New Testament silent where the Old Testament speaks clearly and abundantly. The limited direct evidence for open theology in the New Testament in no way negates the abundance of evidence in the Old.

Hermeneutical Fallacies

In an effort to reconcile Scripture to a preconceived theological or philosophical position, some theologians label every passage of Scripture that attributes repentance, uncertainty, or surprise to God "anthropomorphic." In other words, since theologians already "know" that God cannot change his mind, be uncertain about the outcome of future events, or be surprised by human behavior, passages that run counter to this *a priori* philosophical presupposition are simply accommodations for the "duller folk," God lisping to his people as a nursemaid to a child.[69] "It is assumed that God cannot change his mind; hence verses that explicitly say that he does so can't be accepted at face value."[70]

Dismissing the texts discussed above as anthropomorphic, however, is an "arbitrary and drastic solution that cuts rather than unties the theological knot. A more satisfying solution exists, if the biblical evidence is allowed to speak for itself."[71]

There are many problems with this methodology. First, human beings can only know God in so much as God has revealed himself. Therefore, every description of God in Scripture is an anthropomorphism, for only through anthropomorphisms can humanity comprehend a transcendent God. Even descriptions of God as infinite, *actus purus*, omnipotent and Being itself are anthropomorphic "in that they are human words applied to God."[72]

Thomas Aquinas recognized the inability of man to know God "as he really is," when he said, "we come to know and name God from creatures."[73] In other words, "all of our knowledge of God arises from within the created order."[74] Since all divine revelation is condescension—all our knowledge of God arises from the created order, which God himself transcends—and thereby anthropomorphic—ascribing human actions and characteristics to a non-human being—

> We must believe God's word concerning Himself, and humbly accept such insight as He vouchsafes to give. [We must believe] in Him as He is, and this is the only possible way, by thinking of Him in the aspect in which He presents Himself to us.[75]

To label some passages anthropomorphic and others "literal" is simply impossible because no such distinction exists.[76] All descriptions of God are anthropomorphic or metaphorical. Therefore, if we are to accept Scripture's depiction of God as having any correspondence with reality, we must drop this false dichotomy. Simply put, if God reveals himself as a God who changes his mind or experiences surprise or uncertainty, believers must accept him as such.[77]

In addition, claiming that such passages are simply metaphorical or parabolic does nothing to solve the problem these passages present to traditional theology. All metaphors "must connect with reality at some point if they are to communicate anything meaningful."[78] While metaphors may be non-literal themselves, they serve as colorful descriptors of literal reality.

For example, the phrase, "The President is mad as a hornet," is a metaphorical way of describing the intense literal reality of the President's anger.[79] This statement obviously does not mean that the President of the United States is literally an insect but rather serves to emphasize the intensity of his anger.

This phrase cannot mean, however, that the President appears to be angry, but in reality, he is not angry at all. "Though the use of the metaphor is not literal, there is literalness intended in the relationship to which the metaphor has reference."[80] This is just as true in Scripture as it is anywhere else. Indeed, even the "language of science is often metaphorical."[81] (Consider such terms as the "big bang," "red dwarf," and "black hole.") No one would suggest that the use of metaphorical language negates the literal reality of scientific truth. (Indeed, those who explain away inconvenient passages of Scripture by labeling them anthropomorphic or metaphorical fail to grasp the very meaning and concept of metaphor.)

Of course, the phrase "The President is mad as a hornet" is not a precisely analogous description. Hornets may behave in such a way that appears to resemble the angry behavior of humans, but hornets do not have actual emotions, at least as we understand them. Human language creates this metaphor to describe a literal reality—the President's anger—through a very non-literal expression—hornets do not, as far as we know, actually experience anger.

Similarly, all language about God is analogous. Human beings have nothing with which to compare divine behavior other than human behavior. Therefore, even the most seemingly literal statements about divine behavior are metaphors, for through them Scripture teaches that God behaves in such a way that finds its closest analogy in human conduct. To say God changes his mind is to say that God behaves in such a way that is similar to—though not completely in line with—the way a man behaves when he changes his mind.

Man cannot, however, dissect and explain the mind of God as he can the hornet. Some may argue that God changes his mind from the human perspective only, not from the divine perspective. Such talk, however, is nonsensical because the divine perspective is inaccessible to humanity. Indeed, on what foundation would we attempt to make such a description of it? How closely God's phenomenological behavior corresponds with his ontological reality—or his divine essence—is beyond the realm of human understanding.

Therefore, believers must accept metaphors describing divine behavior as pointing to a literal reality, even if that literal reality to which the metaphor points is only literal from an anthropological perspective. That is, after all, as high as human understanding can ascend. For revelation to maintain coherence, there must be some sort of literal correspondence, however obscure, between the way a human changes his mind, for example, and the way God changes his mind. The two cannot be completely foreign ideas and still make sense.

So, when Scripture describes God as possessing ears (e.g., James 5:4)—for some reason this seems to be a favorite talking point of opponents of open theism—it is speaking metaphorically to point to the reality that God hears and responds to the prayers and cries of his people. Whether or not God literally has ears is of no consequences and not relevant to such passages of Scripture. Such expressions are idiomatic, comparable to a blind man saying, "It's good to see you."[82]

When traditional theologians label passages describing divine repentance as anthropomorphic metaphors, however, they have a hard time affirming to what aspect of reality these metaphors correspond. Those who choose to take such passages metaphorically still must explain the metaphor's meaning and purpose. When traditional theologians end the discussion by declaring such passages metaphorical, they are in reality dismissing the passages as untrue.

These passages, however, have something of great theological significance to say. They cannot be swept under the doctrinal rug because they are inconvenient to systematicians. "God changed his mind," cannot be a metaphorical way of saying, "God cannot change his mind," nor can it be a metaphorical way of saying nothing about God. A metaphor is a colorful description of reality, not a statement contrary to fact. "If God in fact never changes his mind, saying he does so doesn't communicate anything truthful; it is simply inaccurate."[83]

Some could argue that this metaphor does not point to God's changing his mind per se, but rather to the fact that when situations change, God will react accordingly. Reactionary language, however, is the foundation of open theology, and so this route does nothing to dispel the position of open theists.

Many traditional theologians take a slightly different route, claiming such texts describe God phenomenologically, not ontologically. In other words, "It *looks* like God changed his mind, but he *really* didn't."[84] John Calvin, for example, argues that Scripture describing God as changing his mind does so only "because our weakness does not attain to his exalted state." Therefore,

> the description of him that is given to us must be accommodated to our capacity so that we may understand it....[This] mode of accommodation is for him to represent himself to us not as he is himself, but as he seems to us.[85]

Yet the self-defeating nature of this methodology is obvious. If our "weakness" requires God's accommodation, how is that Calvin is capable of looking past that accommodation? "Calvin apparently believes that *his* 'weakness' does not preclude *him* from attaining to God's 'exalted state.'"[86] Indeed, he not only believes he has achieved a level of understanding beyond that which God has provided in Scripture but also attempts to communicate this understanding to others. If God felt humanity incapable of grasping this exalted state of which Calvin speaks, who is Calvin to attempt to circumvent God's judgment on the matter?[87]

Furthermore, if Calvin is able to obtain this level of understanding and then teach it to others, it undermines the entire premise of his argument. God obviously does not have to accommodate himself to us because Calvin is able to understand, and, indeed, the "accommodation" hinders, rather than enhances, our understanding of God. "Otherwise Calvin wouldn't have to work so hard to make sure we do *not* understand that God changes his mind when God himself tells us that he does."[88]

Furthermore, nothing in the text even vaguely implies that Calvin's assessment is true. Rather, Scripture puts forward in very simple terms that God does in fact change his mind, experience surprise and grief, and wonder about the outcome of future events. There is simply no real reason to interpret Scripture's language in such passages any less literally—always a precarious word when interpreting Scripture—than language used elsewhere to support traditional theology.[89]

Dismissing such passages is simply an example of philosophy driving exegesis rather than the other way around.[90] The classical theologian's reluctance to concede the validity of these texts, particularly texts arguing that God can in fact change his mind, leave many frustrated. If God wanted to tell us that he actually sometimes does change his mind, how could he say it any more clearly than he does in these passages?[91] If passages attesting to divine repentance don't "teach us that God can truly change his intentions, what would a passage that *did* teach this look like?"[92]

Another dangerous byproduct of this methodology is its creation of a "canon within a canon." Theologians assign authority to texts that seem to support their own preconceived notions of God as describing God "as he truly is," while discarding texts standing in tension with their systematic theology as accommodating metaphors or anthropomorphisms. Protestant evangelical theology ascribes the highest position of authority to Scripture, and yet Scripture itself makes no such distinction. Worse yet, this "hermeneutic would have us believe we are in a better position to know what God is 'really' like than Moses or Jeremiah."[93]

The result is the arbitrary deciding of what is accommodation and what is not, what is anthropomorphic and what is not, and what is authoritative and what is not, thereby undermining all of Scripture. When answering the question, "Can one not eliminate the testimony of any text one chooses simply by assigning it to accommodation?" Kent Sparks describes this halfhazard exegetical method in a manner that should give every believer holding a high view of Scripture pause.

> My answer to this question is straightforward. Every serious reader of the Bible manages to pursue theological coherence by strategically picking and choosing the texts that speak with greatest authority. We disregard one text, such as Exodus 21:20, which would allow us to beat slaves, in preference for another text, such as Luke 6:27, which enjoins us to love others—even our enemies. We subordinate the texts in which God changes his mind or has a physical body to those texts that present God as immutable and impassible. In so doing, we are navigating in an implicit and sometimes unconscious way through the very real diversity of Scripture. Accommodation is simply an explicit theological rationale for what we already do.[94]

Sparks' response demonstrates an understanding of biblical interpretation devastatingly dangerous to sound exegesis. In addition to undermining the evangelical understanding of Scripture by a vague claim that the Bible consistently contradicts itself, this hermeneutical technique allows for the arbitrary picking and choosing of which passages of Scripture carry authority and which do not, creating a kind of cafeteria approach to revelation. This degrades the entirety of Scripture into total irrelevancy.

Furthermore, Spark's pointing to believers' disregarding passages of Scripture that allow a master to beat his slave in favor of passages that call believers to love everyone is an uncomfortable perspective on biblical interpretation. Sparks fails to mention that American Christians in the nineteenth century neglected Scripture that calls believers to love everyone in favor of passages that allow a master to beat his slave. If Sparks' methodology is applied consistently, such an interpretation is no less valid. Or would Sparks have us believe that the proper interpretation of Scripture is to be determined by the prevailing cultural mores at the time? "Evangelicals commonly assert that only 'liberals' revise the Word of God in light of what is 'acceptable' human reason. But clearly evangelicals are not immune from this practice."[95]

When theologians do not allow Scripture to speak for itself, it simply becomes a tool to oblige preconceived philosophical and theological beliefs, rather than serving as the basis for those beliefs. This is the method of liberal Protestantism, not evangelicalism. Either Scripture is completely and totally authoritative or it is not. Picking and choosing what is reliable and what is not undermines the integrity of all of Scripture.

Traditional theologians would quickly realize the weakness of their own hermeneutical method if openness proponents began to utilize it themselves. If John Sanders explained 1 Samuel 15:29 (addressed below) by saying, "We know, as made evident from the current openness-classical debate, that there are many weak minded individuals who simply do not have the intellectual fortitude to believe in a God who can change his mind. This passage is simply an accommodation to those individuals. We, however, being of stronger intellect, know that God can indeed change his mind, and so this Scripture does not apply to us. It only describes God as he appears to be, not as he really is."

Of course, traditional theologians would rightly chide Sanders for his weak exegetical method. Evangelical theology demands its adherents to accept Scripture's teaching about God, no matter how uncomfortable those teachings may be. "We need to embrace the picture of God that emerges from the biblical revelation, not reject it because it doesn't fit with our philosophical construct of God built on prepositional grounds."[96]

Methods proposed by classical theologians to deal with those texts running counter to their philosophical and systematic understanding of the nature of God create severe problems of textual and theological coherence.

> The problem with all such solutions as to how to use the Bible is that they belittle the Bible and exalt something else. Basically they imply—and this is what I mean when I say that they offer too low a view of scripture—that God has, after all, given us the wrong sort of book and it is our job to turn it into the right sort of book by engaging in these hermeneutical moves, translation procedures or whatever. They imply that the real place where God has revealed himself—the real locus of authority and revelation—is, in fact, somewhere else; somewhere else in the past in an event that once took place, or somewhere else in a timeless sphere which is not really hooked into our world at all or touches it tangentially, or somewhere in the present in "my own experience", or somewhere in the future in some great act which is yet to come. And such views, I suggest, rely very heavily on either tradition (including evangelical

tradition) or reason, often playing off one against the other, and lurching away from scripture into something else.[97]

Affirming Exhaustive Divine Foreknowledge

While an overabundance of biblical evidence exists to support the open model of God, there are passages that seem to stand in tension with its teachings. To determine the compatibility of openness with evangelicalism, we must determine whether or not open theists have been able to offer adequate explanations of these problem passages that are consistent with a high view of Scripture.

1 Samuel 15:29

Twenty-four times in the Old Testament either the narrator or God himself says that God changes his mind. 1 Samuel 15:29 and Numbers 23:19 (discussed below) are the only two instances in which characters in the biblical story explicitly claim that God cannot change his mind.[98]

Traditional theologians such as Bruce Ware, eager to deny the possibility of divine repentance, jump on these two passages as describing God as he really is, while claiming that the other twenty-four accounts of God's mutability are anthropomorphic metaphors, describing God as he appears to be. Considering the previous discussion, this interpretation is problematic at best, and so a close analysis of the texts in question is necessary to come to a more coherent explanation.

In 1 Samuel 15:29, after telling Saul that God had rejected him as king, the prophet Samuel says, "He who is the Glory of Israel does not lie or change his mind; for he is not a man, that he should change his mind." While at first glance this appears to be an unequivocal denial of God's ability to change his mind, read in context, this passage makes no such assertion.

Both before and after this verse, the passage uses the same Hebrew word for "change his mind" in this verse to say that Yahweh regrets making Saul king over Israel (vv. 11, 35). Therefore, in a matter of verses, the passage literally reads, "I *repent* that I made Saul king…He who is the glory of Israel does not lie or *repent*…Yahweh *repented* that he had made Saul king over Israel."[99]

Some classical theologians have argued that a switch between literal and anthropomorphic or ontological and phenomenological must be assumed because otherwise the Bible contradicts itself within a matter of verses. For example, Norma Geisler argues that it is necessary to distinguish between those passages which are literal in the metaphysical sense and those passages which are not because this "same text speaks of God as repenting and not repenting, thus making it necessary to interpret at least one of these instances as non-literal."[100]

Unfortunately, Geisler determines which passages are literal and which are not based on his own philosophical presuppositions. (Of course, this begs the further question, to what extent can we ever use the word "literally" in its literal sense when speaking about God?)

Bruce Ware, in agreement with John Calvin, says, "A given ascription to God may rightly be understood as anthropomorphic when Scripture clearly presents God as transcending the very human or finite features it elsewhere attributes to him."[101] In other words, passages that describe God's changing his mind are non-literal descriptions of God, but passages that teach that God cannot change his mind because he is not human are declarations of metaphysical reality. Calvin and Ware both use this argument to dismiss the numerous passages of Scripture that teach God can change his mind in favor of the two passages that teach he cannot.

Yet, Hosea 11:8-9 undermines Ware's argument. After declaring his intention to bring devastation and ruin upon Israel for her sins, God breaks the flow of declarations of judgment with a lament of love for his people.

> How can I give you up, Ephraim? How can I hand you over, Israel? How can I treat you like Admah? How can I make you like Zeboiim? *My heart is changed within me*; all my compassion is aroused. I will not carry out my fierce anger, nor will I turn and devastate Ephraim. For I am God, and not man—the Holy One among you. I will not come in wrath (emphasis added).

While traditional theologians point to passages that teach that God cannot repent because he is not a man, this passage, using the same Hebrew word for "repent" used in the previously discussed passages, teaches that God *does* repent because he is not a man. This, according to Bruce Ware's hermeneutical methodology, affirms God's ability to change his mind as a ontological reality.

Contrary to traditional explanations, read in light of 1 Samuel 13:13-14, which explains that God had intended to bless Saul but must now judge him instead, 1 Samuel 15:29 is a demonstration, and not a negation, of God's ability to change his mind. Sound hermeneutics do not allow interpreters to take the two surrounding verses describing God's repentance figuratively—as if that would solve the problem—and verse 29 literally, simply because it better fits traditional presuppositions. There is no indication of any switch between literal and figurative within the text. Indeed, there is no need for such a switch because, read in context, there are no contradictions in this passage, even if all three verses are equally "literal."[102]

More troublesome to this traditional interpretation is Samuel's all night prayer vigil the previous night during which he pleads with God to reverse his decision to reject Saul as king. This act demonstrates Samuel's belief that God is at least capable of changing his mind.[103] In fact, though "Samuel was not successful in his intercession on Saul's behalf, the point is still made that God, through the announcement of his decision, had given Samuel the opportunity to respond to that decision before it became irrevocable."[104]

After unsuccessfully trying to convince God to change his mind, however, Samuel concludes that in this instance, God *will* not change his mind. The distinction between "cannot" and "will not" is significant. Elsewhere God declares, "I *will not* change my mind" (Ezek 24:14; Zech 8:14; emphasis added), and by doing so provides exceptions that prove the rule. After all, what purpose could God have in saying he will not change his mind in a certain instance if he could not possibly do so anyway?[105] "In its context the teaching is clear: God reserves the right to alter his plans in response to human initiative, and it is also the divine right not to alter an alteration."[106]

Perhaps if Saul had humbled himself and repented, God would have changed his mind and rescinded his judgment on Saul, but unfortunately, Saul gives God no good reason to reverse his decision. Unlike fickle humans, God will not change his mind for any reasons that are inconsistent with his holy nature. That does not preclude his ability to do so, however, for reasons that are consonant with the divine character.[107]

The point of this passage is not that God is incapable of changing his mind but rather that, unlike a man, he is not plagued with uncertainty, waffling and wavering in his decisions. Yahweh is bold and decisive in his pronouncements.

Numbers 23:19

> God is not a man, that he should lie, nor a son of man, that he should change his mind. Does he speak and then not act? Does he promise and not fulfill?

In the surrounding context of this verse, Balak attempts to pay Balaam to prophecy against the Israelites, but Yahweh lets Balak know that he "is not a man, that he should lie, nor a son of man, that he should change his mind" (Num 23:19). In other words, Yahweh, the true God, "is not like a human being who can lie when it's profitable or a mortal who will change his mind for the sake of convenience."[108]

Yahweh is unequivocally clear that he is a God who will not change his mind for the reasons Balak wants him to do so. This is not a universal statement of God's inability to change his mind (as the rest of the Pentateuch demonstrates); it is simply a statement of divine character and integrity. Indeed, the verse itself makes its pronouncement regarding Yahweh's ability to change his mind in connection with his keeping his promises—

"Does he promise and not fulfill?" It does not seek to answer the questions those involved with the openness debate are asking. (In addition, the evil character of the man speaking these words may also call into question whether the author intended this verse to serve as a universal statement of objective theological truth.)

These two statements from 1 Samuel and Numbers, commonly utilized by traditional theologians to deny the reality of divine repentance, do not pose a serious obstacle to open theism as a legitimate expression of evangelical theology. In fact, "there is no good reason to interpret these two passages more literally than those that teach us God can and does change his mind."[109] When read in context, there is no conflict to be resolved. "No strained reinterpretation of a major motif of Scripture is needed."[110]

Psalm 139

This passage seems to stand in direct contradiction to open theology, particularly verse 4. "Before a word is on my tongue you know it completely, O Yahweh." This psalm, however, simply suggests that Yahweh is so acquainted with the psalmist that he knows the psalmist's thoughts before they become speech. "Such divine knowledge is indeed wonderful, unattainable by the human (v. 6), but not necessarily limitless with respect to the future."[111] After all, a man will often say of a wife or girlfriend, "She knows what I'm going to say before I say it," or "We complete each other's sentences." The meaning of these phrases is to express the level of intimacy the two lovers share, not to attribute foreknowledge of future events to a significant other.

Most troubling to the open view, however, is verse 16. "All the days ordained for me were written in your book before one of them came to be." This is poetic literature, however, not an epistle or narrative, calling its usefulness for settling doctrinal disputes into question. "The point of this passage is to poetically express God's care for the psalmist from his conception, not to resolve metaphysical disputes regarding the nature of the future."[112] We pervert Scripture when we force it to answer questions the text is not asking.

Furthermore, the Hebrew here is ambiguous; what is formed and written in the book is unclear. It could be the days or it could be the parts of the body. The King James Version, for example, reads, "Thine eyes did see my substance, yet being unperfect; and in thy book *all my members* were written, which in continuance were fashioned, when as yet there was none of them." Though slightly awkward, this rendering is more consistent with the context, being as the preceding verse describes the formation of the psalmist's body in his mother's womb.[113] This interpretation is thus a valid one and leaves the compatibility of Scripture and open theism unthreatened.

Isaiah 40-55

This lengthy Old Testament passage magnifies God's unfathomable understanding (40:28) and his prediction of the future (e.g., 24:9; 46:10-11), a quality distinguishing Yahweh from the other gods (e.g., 41:21-23; 44:7-8). This passage, however, only declares God's ability to do whatever it is he pleases, unilaterally determining the future by his own actions should he so choose. "Most future-oriented prophetic texts are open-ended, dependent in some way on human response, and hence indeterminate."[114] This passage proclaims God's omnipotence and infinite intelligence. It does not address God's exhaustive foreknowledge of all future events in the sense applicable to the openness-classical debate.

Prophecy

The seemingly greatest obstacle to the open model of God is prophecy, for it is prophecy that most strongly suggests exhaustive divine foreknowledge. In light of the strong biblical evidence in support of the open model of God, however, the classical understanding of prophecy and how it relates to divine foreknowledge seems suspect.

According to the open theist, there are only three types of prophetic passages in Scripture: (1) those that are conditioned upon human behavior, such as God's various pronouncements against Israel, (2) those that are predictions based on existing trends, such as God's prediction that Pharaoh will not willingly release the Israelites from bondage, and (3) those describing what God himself intents to bring about, such as the restoration of creation at Christ's second coming. All three are consistent with the tenets of open theism.[115]

The presence of the first type of prophetic passage throughout Scripture lends greater credence to the open theist's understanding of prophecy. Indeed, the open theist would suggest that many passages that appear to be unconditional and unequivocal statements of future events are in fact conditional prophecies. Therefore, many prophetic passages that do not appear to be conditioned upon human behavior in fact are.

For example, in the book of Jonah, God unambiguously declares the coming destruction of Nineveh. Yet the people repent and destruction is averted. Despite its appearing unconditional, this prophecy was clearly conditioned on the people's response. Had the people of Nineveh not repented, the city would have been destroyed, and the prophecy would have appeared unconditional.

The conditional nature of the prophecy is obvious only because it did not come to pass. It stands to reason, therefore, that many prophecies that seem unconditional appear as such only because the conditions necessary for God to alter his plans were not met.[116] Elijah's seemingly unqualified prophecy against King Ahab in 1 Kings 21:17-24 (discussed above) and its subsequent delay is another example of the conditional nature of seemingly unconditional prophecies.

With regard to the second category, the doctrine of omniscience—that is, that God possesses complete and perfect knowledge of all of reality—necessitates that God possesses complete knowledge of the past and present and the aspects of the future the past and present necessitate as inevitabilities, thereby giving him an extraordinary ability to predict aspects of the future that he chooses to leave open.

With regard to the third category, the doctrine of divine omnipotence teaches that God is able to bring about whatever he wills by simple divine decree, regardless of his possession of exhaustive foreknowledge of future events. While prophecy—as it is commonly understood—does seem to suggest exhaustive divine foreknowledge, it does not require it, allowing the open theist to affirm the authority of all of Scripture, including prophecy.

1 Kings 13, however, seems to present a major problem to the open model of God. Here, a prophet declares that a son of David named Josiah will defile the altar of Jeroboam at Bethel. Under the principle of omnipotence, however, open theists are able to claim God's ability to raise up a man name Josiah to fulfill this prophecy without having simple foreknowledge of the events.[117]

Open theology does not teach that all aspects of the future are open to God, but rather only those—limited—aspects which he chooses to leave open. Therefore, even leaving aside issues of textual criticism—which may suggest that the name Josiah was inserted into the text at a later date following the reforms of that king—God could have decided that a man named Josiah would bring about reforms and then by his sheer omnipotence brought it to pass. The nature of the open model of God allows for fixed aspects of the future, but a demonstration of just one aspect of the future remaining open devastates the traditional position.

While this prophecy is indeed an incredible one, read in context, it actually supports the open model of God. What's most interesting about this prophecy, is verse 33. "After this event Jeroboam did not return from his evil way..." This verse suggests that the purpose of the prophecy was to provoke Jeroboam to repentance. In fact, the prophecy was issued only in response to Jeroboam's wickedness, which itself necessitated a change in the divine plan.

In 1 Kings 11, Yahweh promises to make Jeroboam's dynasty as enduring as David's if he will simply follow after Yahweh with his whole heart. Yahweh's original hope was to bless Jeroboam, not curse him. This prophecy of judgment against Jeroboam represents a shift from an earlier prophetic promise, making its usefulness as a means to prove exhaustive divine foreknowledge minimal if not self-defeating.

Some opponents of open theism point to God's various declarations through the prophets that the people will not heed the call to repentance. While the people do in fact fail to respond appropriately, it is very different to say that God, possessing perfect knowledge of the people and their character, accurately predicted that they would not repent than it is to say that God knew before the creation of the world that the people of Israel would rebel against him and refuse to repent. Furthermore, if God really knew with absolute certainty that the people would not repent and held no hope to the contrary, what sense do his calls to repentance make? Indeed, as discussed above, God seems to hold a genuine hope that the people will indeed repent.[118]

Turning to what is considered the epitome of prophecy within much of evangelicalism, it is unnecessary to explore in depth the implications of the Apocalypse of John within the openness debate. Considering the numerous interpretations of the Book of Revelation that deny its usefulness as a roadmap of future events, particularly the preterist and idealist positions—and in some ways, the historical premillennialist position—there is no real need to address its usefulness in debunking open theism as a valid evangelical interpretation. Those who consider Revelation to be an apocalyptic description of events now past or simply a description of the ongoing battle between good and evil that will culminated in Christ's victory over Satan are not placed outside the evangelical fold. Therefore, Revelation does not pose a serious threat to open theist-evangelical compatibility.

In light of 2 Peter 3, the usefulness of the return of Christ as a point in arguing for exhaustive divine foreknowledge also seems questionable at best.

> The Lord is not slow in keeping his promise, as some understand slowness. He is patient with you, not wanting anyone to perish, but everyone to come to repentance. But the day of the Lord will come like a thief…You ought to live holy and godly lives as you look forward to the day of God and speed its coming (vv. 9-11).

This passage actually teaches that believers can hasten the Lord's coming, implying that how Christians spread and people respond to the gospel has an effect on the timing of Christ's return. This stands in direct contradiction to the traditional understanding that the timing of the return of Christ is eternally fixed. "What is the point of talking about God's delay due to his patience or encouraging believers to speed up Christ's return by how they live if in reality the exact time has been settled from all eternity?"[119]

When Jesus says, "No one knows about that day or hour, not even the angels in heaven, nor the Son, but only the Father," (Mark 13:32), he is saying that determining the date is the Father's responsibility, not that he has already set the date. To borrow an analogy from Greg Boyd, the Father knows the hour of Christ's return in the same way an earthly father knows when his daughter is old enough to date. This doesn't mean he has a date fixed in his mind; only that he'll know when the right time has come. In the same way a daughter can hasten that day by demonstrating maturity, so can the church also, according to 2 Peter 3, hasten the Lord's return by obediently spreading the gospel.[120]

Many also point to messianic prophecies as a demonstration of God's exhaustive foreknowledge of future events. Again, according to open theology, God in his omnipotence can bring about whatever he wishes. If he desired to fulfill these messianic prophecies in Christ, he could have, with or without exhaustive foreknowledge of future events.

Messianic prophecies, however, create a much smaller problem than may appear. "Evangelicals tend to read more into prophecy than is actually there. This is especially true concerning messianic prophecy, which is a late development in the Old Testament."[121] Considering the gospel writers' application of Scripture to Christ, even where it clearly does not fit the context of the original writings, it is more accurate to view these prophecies as illustrative rather than predictive. "In this view, New Testament authors cite certain Old Testament passages to note that Jesus' life and death *illustrate* what the passages are about, not to show that Jesus' life *had* to unfold in a particular manner."[122] Consider, for example, the prediction of Judas' betrayal of Christ.

> If this view is accepted, one could argue that no one *had* to betray Jesus. But given the fact that by the time of the Last Supper it was certain Judas was going to betray Jesus, David's betrayal by a close friend a thousand years earlier (Ps. 41:9) could now be cited as an inspired anticipation of what Jesus was going to go through. Declaring his knowledge of this inspired pattern would help demonstrate Jesus' divinity and strengthen the faith of his disciples.[123]

The reference to Zechariah 11:12-13 in Matthew 27:9 with regard to Judas' betrayal further demonstrates this point. Neither Zechariah nor Jeremiah 19 and 32, which are also referenced, have any kind of prophetic resemblance to the chief priests' using the money Judas returned to buy a field. The gospel writers' utilization of these passages is incoherent if they are understood to be predictive of future events. Understanding their use of these passages as illustrative of Christ's life and ministry, however, brings the real purpose of the Gospel writers into focus.

Peter's Denial

Opponents of open theism utilize Christ's prediction of Peter's denial (Matt 26:33-35) and its subsequent fulfillment to demonstrate that God possesses exhaustive foreknowledge of future events, even the free acts of individuals. This, of course, would contradict the premise of open theism.

The obvious point of this passage, however, is not that God possesses exhaustive foreknowledge of the future actions of free agents. The focus of this passage is Peter's misunderstanding of the nature of Jesus' messiahship. Jesus is pointing out to Peter that his loyalty will fail when he realizes his hopes for a political Messiah are in vain, as he is ill prepared to handle circumstances contrary to his expectations.[124]

Jesus knew that those hopes of Peter would be dashed that very night, and he knew that Satan had asked permission to test Peter's faith (Luke 22:31). Indeed, having succeeded with Judas, Jesus knew that Satan was turning to destroy the faith of the remaining disciples. Peter's place as the leader of the apostles, a role of which the gospel readers would have been well aware, makes him the perfect focal point to demonstrate the failure of all of the apostles during Christ's passion.[125] This passage is not a demonstration of God's knowledge of Peter's future free acts, but rather God's perfect knowledge of Peter himself.

The exact number of times Peter denies Christ is also of little significance. The point is not that Christ is supernaturally predicting that Peter would encounter three chances to deny the Lord and would fail all three times. The point is that Peter—and all the disciples—would fully and completely denounce their allegiance to Christ before dawn.

With this in mind, it is possible that the number as well as the corresponding failures simply serve as a common biblical literary device to annunciate this point. More likely, however, God, possessing complete knowledge of present events, could easily have perfectly predicted the nature and the number of Peter's failure in a matter of hours—Christ is not predicting Peter's failure in fifty years—based on an inevitable future resulting from present conditions.

The Predestined and the Elect

Many New Testament passages refer to God's predestining and foreknowing the church (e.g., Eph 1:4; 2 Tim 1:9). These passages most likely refer to the predestining of the existence of the church and God's foreordained plans in dealing with members of that church. They do not teach that God predestined which individuals would be a part of that church and which would not.

Consider this analogy: Suppose you attend a seminar in which a certain video is shown. You might ask the instructor, "When was it decided (predestined) that we'd watch this video?" To which the instructor might respond, "It was decided six months ago that you'd watch this video." Note that it was not decided six months ago that *you individually* would watch this video. What was decided was that *anyone who took this seminar* would watch this video. Now that you have chosen to be part of this seminar, what was predestined for the seminar applies to you. You can now say, "It was decided six months ago that *we* would watch this video."[126]

These passages pose no serious threat to open theology. In fact, Scripture elsewhere affirms that were the salvation of individuals up to God alone, he would predestine all for salvation (e.g., 1 Tim 2:4; 2 Peter 3:9), further validating this method of interpreting passages regarding the predestined and the elect. Arguing that God both desires all to be saved and yet predestines only some to salvation is not a paradox; it is simply incoherent. Paradox is not synonymous with logical contradiction.

Such strenuous means of dealing with the issue of the predestined church are unnecessary in light of the reasonable explanation open theism offers. God gave humanity free will, and only those who choose to be "in Christ" are predestined to be "holy and blameless before him in love."[127]

Romans 9-11

No passage has been utilized more frequently or with more force for the cause of proving exhaustive divine foreknowledge in general—and Calvinism in particular—than Romans 9-11. At first glance, this passage seems to present a clear statement that God's predestines some for salvation and others for eternal damnation.[128] This, of course, would completely undermine open theology—and Arminian thought—and consequently place it at odds with the biblical witness. Therefore, in order to demonstrate the compatibility of openness and evangelicalism, an in-depth look at Romans 9-11 is required.

Romans 9-11 must be read in context. This passage addresses the church, not individual salvation, and so it has little bearing on the openness debate. Romans 9-11 speaks about the relationship between Jews and Gentiles, and has little to do with the individual believer and his or her eternal destiny. Other Pauline writings help put this passage into its proper context.

The entire Pauline corpus documents the apostle's struggle to ascertain the proper place of the Gentile believers among the followers of the Jewish Messiah. As Christianity spread, attempts to find the position of the Gentiles within a Jewish messianic movement gave way to a struggle to find the place of the Jewish believers within a predominately Gentile church.

Throughout his letters, Paul's inability to escape the tension created by a people of God brought together across historical and ethnic lines is well documented. In what seemed like a radical step to many Jewish believers of his time, Paul recognized the equality Jews and Gentiles held before God and pointed to a time when the ethnic distinctions will disappear, when the "fullness of the Gentiles" will come to salvation and "all Israel will be saved."

The concept of corporate election played heavily in Israelite theology. Israel understood herself to be a special nation, chosen by God as an instrument by which he would restore the fallen world. Israel based this confidence on the divine covenant rooted in God's promises to the patriarchs (cf. Gen 12; 15; 17; 22), which elevated her to a place of honor among the other nations (Deut 25:15, 17-19).

Israel understood Abraham and his seed to be the divine answer to Adam's sin, and so she saw herself as the true Adamic community, the means by which, according to the Old Testament prophets, God would relate to the rest of the world.[129] While the nature of this understanding of herself developed over time, the basic concept appears throughout Israelite history. The nation of Israel was to serve as the world's priest. This election to which Paul alludes in Romans 9-11 is the election of the nation of Israel, not of individuals.

> Isaiah and Micah speak of Zion as the place to which the nations would come, and of Israel's task as being their light (cf. Isa 2:2-5; 42:6; 49:6; 51:4; Mic 4:1-5). The prophets who look ahead to the restoration of Jerusalem and the rebuilding of the temple see in this event the refounding of the Garden of Eden; Ezekiel envisages rivers flowing out to water and healing the rest of the world (cf. Ezek 40-7, especially 47:7-12), Zephaniah imagines the nations looking on in admiration as YHWH restores the fortunes of his people (Zeph 3:20), and Zechariah (who imitates Ezekiel's idea of rivers) sees the restoration of Jerusalem as the signal for YHWH to become king over all the world, so that the nations will come to Jerusalem to keep the Jewish festivals (Zech 14:8-19)....Israel is to be the true people of the one God, whose fortunes are the key to those of the whole world.[130]

Isaiah's message most explicitly addresses God's purpose in Israel's election: "It is too small a thing for you to be my servant to restore the tribes of Jacob and bring back those of Israel I have kept. I will also make you a light to the Gentiles, that you may bring my salvation to the ends of the earth" (Isa 49:6). God's ultimate purpose in Israel's election was to reconcile all nations to himself.[131] God chose Israel from "all the families of the earth"

(Amos 3:2) so that all the nations would be blessed through her (Gen 12:3),[132] making it clear that "the election of Israel was a means and not the end of God's purpose in the world....Israel became the vehicle by which God's whole creation was to be reconciled to its creator."[133]

Israel, however, was prone to forget the purpose of her election, particularly after enduring trials and persecutions at the hands of foreign oppressors. Contrary to God's revealed objective, the Jews often saw themselves as the means by which God would deliver wrath, not mercy, to the nations. Consider the writings of the *Psalms of Solomon*:

> See, Lord, and raise up for them their king, the Son of David, to rule over your servant Israel...Undergird him with the strength to destroy the unrighteous rulers, to purge Jerusalem from gentiles who trample her to destruction; in wisdom and in righteousness to drive out the sinners from the inheritance; to smash the arrogance of sinners like a potter's jar; to shatter all their substance with an iron rod; to destroy the unlawful nations with the word of his mouth...(*Pss Sol* 17:21-24).[134]

As Israelite history progressed, her understanding of election for purpose gave way to a delight in election as status. The Jews perverted the meaning of their election, elevating themselves above the Gentiles.[135] They failed to realize that their election did not indicate a lack of divine interest in the other nations.[136] In fact, the very opposite was true. Israel's election was the clearest indication that God was *greatly* interested in all peoples.

This misunderstanding of and perverted pride in their election prompted the Jews to place their trust in the Torah as the mark of their status before God. So tied into their understanding of salvation and divine deliverance was the Torah that any concept of deliverance through any other source but Torah was unacceptable to the Jewish mind. The message of Jesus Christ was repugnant to the Jews because it claimed an outworking of God's salvation apart from Torah. To have the Torah was to be a Jew and to be a Jew was to be blessed of God. The Torah therefore functioned as a mark of superiority.[137]

The life of the pre-Christian Paul vividly demonstrates this inwardly focused nationalistic pride. Indeed, the terms Paul uses to describe his attacks on the church in Galatians 1:13 reflect his previous zeal for the law: the Greek words for "persecute" and "destroy" that Paul utilizes parallel the language describing the violent measures employed by the Jews against apostates, whose behavior aligned them with the nations (e.g., Num 25:1-5, 25:6-15; 1 Macc 2:23-28, 42-48; 2 Macc 6:13; IQS 9:22; IQM 7:5; 10:2-5; IOH 14:13-15; *Pss Sol* 17:21-46; Bar 4:25). Evidently, the "pre-Christian Paul agreed with the traditional telling of the story of Israel: if Jews will embrace the Torah wholeheartedly, then God will restore her to the covenantal blessings" (cf. Gal 1:13-14; Phil 3:4-6).[138] The gospel message of Jesus, with its criticisms of the Torah and the Temple, was therefore unacceptable.[139]

As the apostle to the Gentiles, however, Paul is forced to reevaluate his ethnocentric understanding of election. In Romans, Paul argues that the Jews have misunderstood the purpose of their election and have therefore missed God's overarching plan of salvation. Just as the Jews often failed to acknowledge God's working in their midst in the Old Testament (cf. Amos 3:6-7), they now refuse to recognize the outworking of God's plan through Jesus Christ and the consequential ingathering of the Gentiles into the people of God apart from the Torah. The Jews put their faith in their election by God but failed to understand the purpose of that election: to bring the "nonelect" into covenantal relationship with God.[140]

Paul began his missionary work among the Jews, but it proved to be a miserable failure. In fact, the Jews often reacted to Paul's message so violently that he was forced to flee for his life (Acts 9:23-25; 13:45; 14:5, 19). Sadly, just as the Jesus movement began gaining steam in Israel and Gentiles began coming to Christ through the ministry of the original—Jewish—apostles, sparking hope for the fulfillment of the Abrahamic promise, Israel rejected her Messiah. Consequently, Paul is forced to abandon his mission among the Jews, bringing the gospel directly to the Gentiles instead (Acts 13:46; 28:28).[141] Ironically, Israel's devotion to Torah resulted in her rejection of her own Messiah, thereby incurring God's wrath[142] and losing access to her ancestral blessings.[143]

As mentioned earlier, some Old Testament and intertestamental writings envision the incoming of Gentiles during the future salvation of Israel (Isa. 2:2-4; 25:6-10; 56:6-8 (cf. 42:67); Micah 4:1-4; Zech. 8:20-23; *Tobit* 13:3; 14:5-7; *1 Enoch* 90:30, 33; 91:14; *Pss. Sol.* 17:31; *Sib. Or.* 3:710-23),[144] but Paul goes so far as to announce the Gentiles to be the recipients of Israel's blessings. He regularly applies Old Testament terminology for Israel to the Christian Gentiles: the Greek word *ekklēsia*, often translated "church" or "assembly" (cf. 1 Thess 1:1; 2 Thess 1:1 with Deut 23:1, 4, 9 LXX); "beloved of God" (cf. 1 Thess 1:4, 2:12; 2 Thess 2:13-14 with Deut 4:37, 7:8, 10:15, 23:5); "called" (cf. 1 Thess 1:4, 2:12; 2 Thess 1:11, 2:14 with Is 41:9, 42:6, 48:12); "saints/sanctified" (c. 1 Thess 4:1-8, 5:23-24; 2 Thess 2:13-14 with Lev 20:24, 26 LXX); "people of the 'spirit' and thus members of the new covenant of obedience to God" (cf. 1 Thess 1:5-6, 4:8 with Ezek 36:25-27 LXX; see also Ezek 11:19, 18:31, 37:14; Jer 31 (LXX 38): 31-34, 32:40, 50:5). [145]

In his letters to the Thessalonians, Paul argues that God has elevated the Gentiles to a status unfamiliar in the Old Testament, while non-Christian Jews have been cast outside God's sphere of covenantal blessings because of their lack of faith.[146] Israel's "assumption of monopoly on divine mercy and of gentile exclusion through disobedience has been turned on its head. Gentile disobedience did *not* disqualify from mercy, and irony of ironies, what did 'qualify' the Gentiles was *Jewish* disobedience."[147]

Paul attacks the Jewish confidence in Torah, pointing to the righteousness credited to the Gentiles, despite their never having followed the Mosaic Law (Rom 9:30).[148] Israel's refusal to acknowledge that her covenant privileges have been extended to all has resulted in the loss of those very privileges she sought to protect. By extending the covenantal blessings to the Gentiles, however, God has accomplished that which was his goal from the very beginning: to make available the covenantal blessings to all the nations.[149] Israel's refusal to accept this step in God's plan because of her devotion to the Torah has, ironically, brought her under the Torah's curses (Phil 3:3).[150]

Therefore, God's bringing the Gentiles into the covenant came as a surprise to the Jews. Paul rejects the notion that Israel's covenantal blessings are accessible to Gentiles only through a conversion to Judaism, pointing to God's election of Isaac and Jacob over Ishmael and Esau respectively as proof that God can show mercy to whomever he wants (Rom 9-11). Therefore, "if God wants to show mercy to the Gentiles by bringing them into the people of God simply by faith in Jesus without the badges of the covenant members, God is free to do it (Rom 9:15-16)."[151] The Jews have no right to object.

This does not teach, as many claim, that God arbitrarily predestines some to hell and others to heaven. This passage says nothing about the predestination of individual eternal destinies; Paul is speaking of God's opening up of the Jewish covenantal blessings to the entire world.

At the heart of the debate is faith, for faith has always been the standard by which God has judged his people. The Jews refused to put their faith in Christ, choosing instead to rely on the law of Moses (Rom 10:3),[152] while the Gentiles chose to put their faith only in the crucified Christ, and so, ironically, now enjoy the traditional Deuteronomic blessings.[153]

For Paul, "the Gentiles are no longer a lesser breed without the law, either to be exterminated or to come in at the last to learn from Israel and in effect to acknowledge Zion's primacy" (cf. Isa 2:2-3; *Pss Sol* 17:33-35; *Sib Or* 3.710-20).[154] Indeed, Paul's comments throughout the Pauline corpus indicate that Israel as the people of God has been reinterpreted along spiritual, not national or ethnic lines.[155] Consequently, believing Gentiles now share in Israel's blessings.[156]

The Gentiles, however, have become arrogant because of their election in Christ, paralleling the arrogance of the Jews that Paul so intensely despised. Romans 9-11, so often misinterpreted to be an exposition on individual predestination, addresses concerns over Israel's election.

Paul affirms the *conditionality* of the main thing Calvinists want to view *unconditionally*, namely, salvation! This is clear from his discussion of the eternal destiny of individual Jews. Any who are rejected as far as salvation is concerned are rejected because of personal unbelief (Rom 9:32; 11:20). Likewise, any Jew can be saved by accepting Jesus as the Messiah (10:13-17; 11:23-24). In fact God is pictured as constantly pleading with Israel to come to him, but they remain disobedient and obstinate (10:21).[157]

"The danger was that a predominantly Gentile church, placing its faith in Jesus, would become arrogant, would regard ethnic Israel as hopeless and would find a mission to the Jews unnecessary."[158] Paul is seeking to dismiss the notion that God's purposes for Israel have failed, arguing instead that God is keeping his promise to Abraham and faithfully accomplishing his mission with Israel.

Romans 9-11, therefore, cannot be understood in the traditional Calvinist approach as an exposition on predestination. Rather, these three chapters address God's covenantal faithfulness,[159] not meticulous divine control of the individual's eternal destiny. Paul is talking about Israel and the nations, not individuals. This is very significant for the openness debate—and indeed, the debate between Calvinism and traditional Arminianism—because it allows for a viable interpretation of Romans 9-11 that avoids an affirmation of individual predestination and comprehensive divine foreknowledge.

This is not to say, however, individuals are not implicated. Paul could not have imagined an eschatological Israel totally devoid of historical Israel,[160] which of course, requires the salvation of individual Israelites. The focus nevertheless remains on the overall relationship between Jews and Gentiles as distinct groups.

In Paul's understanding, certain legal theological factors have to be considered before declaring that the Gentiles have completely usurped Israel's position. For example, if God has made promises to Israel, those promises cannot be nullified without first breaking the covenant.[161]

Since God's righteousness is determined by his faithfulness to his covenantal commitments, the state of the covenant between God and Israel is of the utmost importance.[162] Paul argues that "Gentiles have too easily presumed on their access to the heritage of Israel to which they have no inherent right."[163] God's faithfulness—and nothing else—necessitates that he remain committed to ethnic Israel, whether she cooperates or not.[164]

In his olive tree metaphor (Rom 11:17-24), Paul maintains only one tree, never allowing for its removal or replacement by another. There is only one tree, and therefore only one people of God: Israel.[165] "Christian identity is unavoidably corporate and bound up with the identity of Israel."[166] The Gentile branches have been grafted into the tree (Rom 11:17), but they do not constitute a new growth. In their being grafted in, the Gentiles share in Israel's covenant status, but only because they have been made a part of, not replaced, Israel.[167] "This makes it perfectly clear that the church of Jesus Christ lives from the root and the trunk of the Old Testament Israel."[168]

Furthermore, while the breaking off of the natural branches made room for the Gentiles to share in Israel's covenant status (Rom 11:19-20), "that did not reverse the line of dependence of all branches on the historical roots" (Rom 11:8).[169] God's promises to Israel are irrevocable (Rom 11:29), and Israel continues to occupy an "inalienable place in the divine economy of salvation."[170] Paul warns the Gentiles that just as unbelieving Jews will eventually be grafted back into the tree (Rom 11:23-24, 26), the Gentile branches can be broken off once more should they fall into unbelief (Rom 11:22).[171] While there are certainly ramifications for the individual, corporate salvific identity is the issue here.

Finally, in Romans 11:25, Paul begins to explain the mystery of God's plan of salvation to the Gentiles with the phrase "in order that you might not be wise in your own estimation." "Wise in your own estimation," refers to the arrogance of ethnic exclusivity,[172] echoing Paul's warning to the Jews in Romans 2:17-24.[173] Paul's use of the Greek word for "mystery" here is reminiscent of apocalyptic literature (cf. LXX Daniel 2:18, 27-30, 47; 1 Enoch 51:3; 103:2; 104:10; IQS 4:18; IQpH 7:5, 8, 14), which usually uses the word to refer to an eschatological event that has already been determined by God.[174]

As an aside, it is important to note that God's predetermining a future event does not contradict open theology, since open theism allows God to predetermine whatever he likes. Only if God predestines *all* future events is open theology contradicted. The open theist can affirm God's ability to bring about the eschatological salvation of Israel without affirming his desire to predestine all events, and by doing so can maintain internal philosophical consistency while preserving the integrity and truth of Scripture.

Returning to the passage at hand, Paul, realizing that their ignorance has caused their arrogance,[175] wants the Gentiles to be knowledgeable of God's plan, so that they will stop thinking of themselves as occupying a higher position than the Jews. Gentiles are only one part of God's greater plan of salvation, a plan which must climax with the salvation of Israel.[176] If the Gentiles could only grasp their position in relation to the Jews within God's purpose, they would have nothing about which to boast.[177]

God is not finished with Israel (Rom 11:25-32). Indeed, nothing less than God's own integrity is at stake, for God's giving of mercy so freely to the Gentiles, while Israel receives none, calls into question God's covenantal faithfulness to Israel. If God's purpose for Israel has been so frustrated, what assurance can the Christian believer have in his or her own position as a member of the people of God?[178]

God's covenantal faithfulness to Israel is currently demonstrated in the preservation of a remnant of believing Jews (Rom 11:3-6). This remnant demonstrates God's unwavering commitment to Israel, pointing to the future salvation of the entire nation.[179] God continues to sustain a remnant of believers within ethnic Israel for no reason other than his covenantal faithfulness. Despite Israel's having rejected her own Messiah and openly demonstrating her hostility to God's gospel (v. 28), God remains faithful to his irrevocable promises to Israel. Herein lies the eschatological tension within Israel:[180] as her present opposition to the gospel makes her an enemy of God,[181] under divine wrath,[182] so also her inheritance of God's promises to the patriarchs simultaneously maintains her position as beloved by God.[183]

The patriarchs occupy an important role within the covenant relationship between God and Israel, not because of anything they did, but because of God's promises to them (Gal 3; Rom 4). Ethnic Israel, therefore, receives God's love for no other reason than God's faithfulness to those promises (Deut 7:7-8).[184] "Israel cannot be written off permanently as God's enemies, since they are still God's elect and beloved people."[185] Indeed, Paul spends almost all of Romans 9 focusing on the divisions within Israel for the sole purpose of demonstrating God's fidelity in the face of an apostate people.[186]

God has maintained a remnant for the sake of his promises to the patriarchs,[187] and it is for the sake of those promises that God eventually will bring salvation to all of Israel (Rom 11:26) and, beyond that, a full inclusion of both Jewish and Gentile humanity (Rom 11:11-24).[188] This passage is a matter of God's remaining faithful despite the unfaithfulness of his people, a statement of his fidelity in the face of a relationship gone bad. It is reminiscent of the prophets, in which Yahweh looked to the hope of the future restoration he would bring about for apostate Israel. Understood in this context, this passage becomes an ally, not an enemy, of open theology.

> I do not want you to be ignorant of this mystery, brothers, so that you may not be conceited: Israel has experienced a hardening in part until the full number of the Gentiles has come in (Rom 11:25).

This verse brings to a climax the discussion that began in verse 11. ("Again I ask: Did they stumble so as to fall beyond recovery? Not at all! Rather, because of their transgression, salvation has come to the Gentiles to make Israel envious.") Paul argues that Israel's current failure does not mean a permanent separation from the covenant promises, but rather that God is temporarily utilizing Israel's hardening in order to further advance the gospel. Israel's "trespass" has allowed the Gentiles to come to salvation through Christ (v. 11), but the Jews will regain their position when their "fullness" overcomes their "defeat" (v. 12) and their acceptance their rejection (v. 15).[189]

In his hardening of Israel, God demonstrates the merciful, not the deterministically arbitrary, nature of his will, which longs for both Jew and Gentile to attain salvation. God's hardening of Israel is reminiscent of his hardening of Pharaoh, whom he hardened in the hope that he would repent of his pride. God is now hardening Israel in her rebellion in the same way, in order to bring about her repentance and, consequently, her salvation (Rom 11:7, 25).[190] "God hardens some in order to save all; he confines all to disobedience in order to show mercy to all."[191]

He does not harden some in order to save some, nor does he confine all to disobedience to show mercy to some. Romans 9-11 demonstrates the understanding of God's mercy and plan of salvation so emphasized by open theism. This hardening gives no support to some kind of double predestination theology. In fact, God's hardening is not a unilateral divine action, but rather a hardening on account of preexisting unbelief (Rom 11:20; cf. Rom 10:3; 11:7, 25).[192] God, therefore, is able to accomplish a dual purpose in his hardening of Israel: bring Gentiles into covenant relationship with himself, and, through this ingathering of Gentiles, bring Israel to repentance. This a clear demonstration of God's resourcefulness, an aspect of the divine nature heavily stressed by open theism.

God, however, has limited the hardening in its scope and time:[193] limited in scope by the remnant which has not been hardened,[194] and limited in time because of Paul's prediction that it will end in the last days,[195] after the full number of Gentiles have entered into the kingdom.[196] This demonstrates the sovereignty of God in bringing about the salvation of his people.

As a river moves toward the sea, so is Israel moving to salvation. While individual water molecules may not make it—some may evaporate, some may be utilized for drinking water, and some may simply splash ashore—the river itself will make it to the sea. This understanding of God's sovereign dealing with corporate entities, while still allowing for individual freedom, fits perfectly into the open model of God.

Yet, while reading Paul's argument, the necessity of Israel's being cast off is not immediately clear. Could not the Gentiles have come into the covenant without the Jews being temporarily thrown out? Paul's answer is no, but only because of the Jewish reaction to the gospel, not because of any predetermined divine plan requiring the hardening of Israel. The ethnocentrism of first century Judaism, reflected both in corporate Israel's rejection of her Messiah and the insistence of some Jewish believers that Gentiles desiring to follow Jesus first become Jews, required that there be a break between the covenant promise and the nation of Israel in order to preserve the integrity of the gospel message.[197]

If the gospel was indeed to be to all nations (Rom 4:16), it had to be removed from Jewish self-understanding. "Without such a break in the continuity of Israel's covenant status any broadening out to embrace the

Gentiles would inevitably have been misunderstood in terms of Jewish self-aggrandizement or religious imperialism."[198] This is even more understandable in light of the ardent Judean nationalism of the time that led to the rebellion against Rome and the subsequent fall of Jerusalem just a few years later.

Consequently, in its initial stage of outreach into the Gentile world, the gospel had to distance itself from Israel, in order that its message of grace might come unfiltered to the Gentiles. Apart from the strings of Jewish self-understanding, the gospel brought to the Gentiles the benefits of the rich covenantal heritage of the Jewish nation apart from a Jewish conversion.[199]

Had the Jews accepted their Messiah and the terms of the new covenant, that is, justification by faith in Christ alone, this casting off of Israel would have been unnecessary. As Acts demonstrates, this throwing off of Israel represents a change in the original plan. It is God's accommodating Israel's disobedience, in order to eventually bring her back to himself. The casting off, therefore, was not an event predestined by God, but rather a change in the divine plan, an accommodation to the situation presented by Israel's disobedience.

Hope remains for Israel because God remains devoted to her. While Paul argues that the first coming of Christ partially fulfilled many of God's promises to Israel, he seems to go to great lengths to emphasize a future salvation for her. He argues that Israel's present situation in salvation history, in light of the low number of Jews coming to faith in Christ, cannot be a complete fulfillment of God's promises.[200]

> And so all Israel will be saved, as it is written: "The deliverer will come from Zion; he will turn godlessness away from Jacob. And this is my covenant with them when I take away their sins." As far as the gospel is concerned, they are enemies on your account, but as far as election is concerned, they are loved on account of the patriarchs, for God's gifts and his call are irrevocable. Just as you who were at one time disobedient to God have now received mercy as a result of their disobedience, so they too have now become disobedient in order that they too may now receive mercy as a result of God's mercy to you. For God has bound all men over to disobedience so that he may have mercy on them all (Rom 11:26-32).

Paul argues in Romans 11 that, while God's mercy to the Jews was highlighted during the period of the Gentiles' hostility to God, the coming of the gospel has emphasized God's mercy to the Gentiles, while the Jews remain hostile to God. This, however, is not the last word for Israel. God will lift up Israel and show her mercy yet again (v. 26).[201]

In 11:32, Paul argues that sin holds all men captive, and only God in his mercy can release them from their prison. Indeed, Paul's argument throughout Romans has been that all human beings, Jew and Gentile alike, are sinful and have access to God's saving grace only through faith in Christ. After pointing to the equality all humanity shares before God in Jesus Christ, Paul predicts the future fullness of both Israel (11:12) and the Gentiles (11:25) within the people of God.[202]

Herein lies the crux of Paul's argument: "only when these two fullnesses are fused together will the new humanity be realized."[203] Paul is not drawing further distinctions between Israel and the Gentiles, as many—particularly dispensationalists—have suggested. Rather, Paul is pointing to a time when the two shall be one, united by their equal status as the people of God.[204] Romans 11:16-25 will permit only one people of God.[205]

Of critical importance and intense debate is Paul's meaning of "all Israel." Throughout his writings, Paul uses the term "Israel" in three distinct ways: to refer to (1) the people of God, including both Jews and Gentiles, (2) those within ethnic Israel who have placed their faith in Christ as Messiah, and (3) the ethnic nation of Israel. Though the first option enjoyed strong support during the early church and post-Reformation periods, the surrounding context makes such an interpretation implausible.[206] While Paul does use the designation "Israel of God" to refer to the church in Galatians 6:16, in Romans, he consistently uses "Israel" to refer to the ethnic or nation Israel, contrasting her with the Gentile nations.[207] Furthermore, Paul is addressing the arrogance of Gentile believers, and so were Paul to use Israel to refer to all believers, he would be contradicting his own purpose.[208]

The second view requires a shift in Paul's use of Israel from verse 25 to verse 26, which is highly unlikely.[209] "It is exegetically impossible to give to 'Israel' in this verse any other denotation than that which belongs to the term throughout this chapter."[210] Therefore, "all Israel" must refer to Israel as a national corporate identity, regardless of the righteousness or sin of individuals within the group.[211] "'All Israel' is a recurring expression in Jewish literature where it need not mean 'every Jew without exception,' but 'Israel as a whole.'"[212]

Unlike many modern symbolic or individualistic understandings, Paul's view on Israel is both historical and communal.[213] In Romans 11:26, "the identity of Israel itself is now in question, precisely because Israel too is caught up in the overlap of the ages, caught between the times." [214] Paul makes a distinction between the identify of ethnic Israel and the Israel of God's plan of salvation, stating that "not all who are descended from Israel are Israel" (9:6). [215]

The temptation to resolve the difficulty of Romans 9-11 by declaring historic Israel to be the old Israel and the Church to be the new Israel is quite enticing and some throughout history have fallen into this trap. This, however, does not adequately address the complexity and nuance of Paul's argument. [216]

Israel's very identity is caught within the eschatological tension that Paul so commonly explores throughout his writings, itself "part of the already-not yet."[217] Choosing the easy interpretive route by cutting short the argument Paul slowly unfolds undermines a proper appreciation of Paul's own answer to the problem posed by God's promises to Israel in light of her rejection of the Messiah.[218]

> Historical Israel has not been denied or rejected. It is in effect the divided "I" of Israel which is being explored. The Israel of ethnic definition and covenant fidelity is still Israel. It may no longer as such be the Israel of God's call. But that statement can be rephrased: it is not yet as such the Israel of God's call. Israel remains caught in the eschatological tension.[219]

Paul argues that God's saving of Israel in the last days will demonstrate his impartiality, lest some conclude that he favors the Gentiles over the Jews. In fact, God has imprisoned all men to disobedience (11:32). The Gentiles received their greatest imprisonment before Christ, while the Jews have received theirs since. To stand in contrast to their few numbers in the present age, however, Jews in great numbers will turn to Christ at the eschaton.[220] Interestingly, this passage demonstrates God's *lack* of partiality when it comes to bringing about salvation. A Calvinistic understanding of predestination suggests the exact opposite.

Paul saw in Deuteronomy 32:21 the answer to the problem of Israel: "They have made Me jealous with what is not God; They have provoked Me to anger with their idols. So I will make them jealous with those who are not a people; I will provoke them to anger with a foolish nation" (NASB). Paul understood the "not a people" and the "foolish nation" to be the Gentiles, the means by which God would provoke Israel to jealousy, and consequently, repentance.[221]

This is particularly ironic when Israel's self-understanding as the means by which God would reconcile a fallen world to himself (discussed above) is considered. God originally wanted to bring his message of salvation to the nations through Israel, but because of Israel's disbelief, he now intends to bring that message to Israel through the nations.[222] To Paul, the salvation of the Gentiles is the means by which God will bring Israel to repentance.[223] Israel's jealousy will be aroused by the realization that her covenantal privileges have been given to the Gentiles (9:4-5), thereby provoking her into accepting Jesus as Messiah.[224]

Paul hopes that by receiving mercy, the Gentile will demonstrate to the Jews that their obedience to the Mosaic law and their zeal for the separateness of Israel is in fact disobedience to the word of faith (10:16, 21). By claiming exclusive rights to God's mercy, Israel has disqualified herself from that very mercy. The disobedience of the Jews has opened mercy up to the Gentiles,[225] which will in turn open up mercy to the Jews by provoking them to holy jealousy.[226] "The pilgrimage of the Gentiles (Is 2:2-5) will not succeed but rather precede the restoration of Israel—the nations do not come because they see Israel's glory, but Israel because she sees the salvation and glory Gentiles have in Christ."[227] This is a clear change in plans, demonstrating that this passage supports, rather than contradicts, open theology.

The interaction between Jews and Gentiles in this back and forth pendulum of divine election will reach its consummation as soon as the gospel spreads to the ends of the inhabited world (10:18) and has resulted in the salvation of the full number of Gentiles.[228] In a grand reversal, Israel is dependent on the Gentiles for her eschatological deliverance, the Gentiles actually preceding the Jews into salvation (Rom 11:12). Yet, the Gentiles also must rely on Israel, for the "final act of all history rests upon the Jews."[229] Therefore, despite the present division of the Church and Israel,

> in the end there can be absolutely no "separate development" because their destinies remain intertwined in the mysterious workings of God's eternal purpose. Thus Israel cannot achieve her restoration until "the fullness of the Gentiles," and the Gentiles cannot participate in the resurrection without the prior restoration of Israel.[230]

"Christian identity is unavoidably corporate and bound up with the identity of Israel."[231] Romans 11, however, does not imply that Paul had a clear understanding of the sequence of events preceding the parousia, nor how Christ's return is related to Israel's conversion (vv. 26-27). "His conviction is simply of a mounting climax with the incoming of the Gentiles as the trigger for the final end in which Israel's conversion, Christ's Parousia, and the final resurrection (v 15) would all be involved."[232]

By using the same Greek word to reference the Gentiles (v. 12) and the Jews (v. 25), Paul implies that the incoming of the Gentiles and the incoming of ethnic Israel would be equivalent. This is not to say Paul is arguing for a one-to-one numerical equivalence, but rather that the two would be sufficiently equivalent to sentence ethnic distinctions to irrelevance.[233] Paul is therefore arguing that "all of Israel will be saved" in the same way that all the Gentiles will be saved, not affirming universalism, but rather pointing to an eschatological ingathering of the Jews that will demonstrate the equal significance of Jews and Gentiles within God's plan of salvation. The percentage of Israel this entails is of little consequence. Paul's ultimate desire is to see the distinction between Jews and Gentiles eliminated, and he argues here that this will finally happen at the eschaton when "all Israel" will be saved.

Even though when Paul refers to Israel in Rom 11:26 he means the historical people bearing that name, he redefines Israel in terms of God's "election" and "call" (11:28, 29), clearly echoing 9:11-12, 24. In the end, the split in Israel will be healed; the distinction between historical Israel and the Israel that is the people of God will be reconciled, disappearing into the "full number" of Jews and Gentiles. "Paul continues to use 'Israel' for historic Israel, but no longer in an excluding way. When 'all Israel' is saved, then the split in the people of God will be healed, the eschatological tension resolved, and the Israel of God made whole."[234]

The point of Romans 9-11 is that the distinction between Jew and Gentile does not reflect God's ideal. God originally made the distinction when he called Abraham, springing forth hope for divine reconciliation to a fallen world. Before this, there were no people of God, but by calling Abraham and his descendants to holiness, God hoped eventually to bring the entire world into covenantal relationship with him, thereby eliminating the need to distinguish between the nations and Israel. Abraham's descendants, however, failed to appreciate this purpose of their divine election. Those who were supposed to be a light unto the nations retreated into national isolation, thwarting God's intention.

So God changed strategies—an understanding very compatible with open theology—bringing the gospel of Jesus Christ directly to the nations (through Jewish apostles). In the process, however, Israel has been left behind. This will not always be the case.

Since God established his relationship with Israel, there has been a gap of faith between Jews and Gentiles. Before Christ, the Jews enjoyed covenant relationship with God, while the Gentiles suffered outside of God's blessings. Since Christ, however, the situation has been reversed, maintaining this Jewish-Gentile division that God never wished to preserve.

Contrary to replacement theology, God is not done with historic Israel. Contrary to dispensational theology, God is not pleased with the Jew-Gentile distinction. Paul points to the day when the outworking of God's saving grace will eliminate the ethnic and historical divisions between Jews and Gentiles, erasing those distinctions forever, and the people of God will stand united as one, as the ethnic titles and historical heritages that once divided melt into oblivion and irrelevancy. "The human body has many parts, but the many parts make up only one body. So it is with the body of Christ" (1 Cor 12:12 NLT).

This is the point of Romans 9-11. This in-depth look at its message was necessary to establish that the utilization of this passage as a tool in arguing for meticulous divine sovereignty, exhaustive divine foreknowledge, or the universal predestination of individuals—all of which explicitly contradict open theism—is inappropriate. This passage therefore offers no serious threat to open theology or to the open theist's claim to the title "evangelical."

Conclusion

While many may find the scriptural interpretations of open theists unconvincing, there is no evidence that their hermeneutical methodology requires their rejection of Scripture's authority—or even its inerrancy or infallibility, for those who wish to use those terms. It is one thing to adamantly disagree with a school of thought's interpretation of Scripture. It is quiet another to attack its view of Scripture itself.

Considering the abundance of texts supporting the open model of God and the lack of an insurmountable scriptural objection to this school of thought, the open model of God should at least be given credence as a valid evangelical position.

Endnotes

[1] Although open theology lacks a strong historical basis, as Greg Boyd points out, it is not the invention of twentieth-century scholarship. Basic tenets of the philosophical foundation of open theology can be found in non-Christian sources, such as Cicero and some medieval Jewish thinkers. It stands in such strong opposition to the Greco-Roman philosophical world into which Christianity initially spread, however, that it is difficult to find in early Christian thought, although it does make a developed appearance in the writings of the fifth-century theologian Calcidius. It also appears in nineteenth-century Methodist writings as well as in African-American Christian thought. The history and development of open theology is outside the scope of this book, however, being as its purpose is to demonstrate the compatibility of open theology and evangelism, not to make an argument for open theology itself. For better or worse, the doctrine of *sola scriptura* and generally accepted tenets of evangelicalism do not require a strong historical basis as a condition of theological legitimacy—as the widespread evangelical acceptance of dispensationalism clearly demonstrates—and so tracing the movement's historical heritage would only distract from the purpose at hand. For a look at the history of open theism see J. Den Boeft, *Calcidius on Fate: His Doctrine and Sources* (New York: Brill, 1997); Gerard Verbeke, *The Presence of Stoicism in Medieval Thought* (Washington, D.C.: Catholic University Press of America, 1983), 82-83; J. H. Waszink, ed., *Timaeus a Calcidio translatus Commentarioque instructus*, 2nd ed., Plato Latinus, vol. 4 (Leiden: Brill, 1975); L. D. McCabe, *Divine Nescience of Future Contingencies as a Necessity* (New York: Philips & Hunt, 1882); idem, *The Foreknowledge of God* (Cincinnati: Cranston & Stowe, 1887); B. Hibbard, *Memoirs of the Life and Travels of B. Hibbard*, 2nd ed. (New York: Piercy & Reed, 1843), 372-414; Major Jones, *The Color of God in Afro-American Thought* (Macon, Georgia: Mercer Press, 1987), 95. (List of sources provided by Greg Boyd in his book *God of the Possible*.)

[2] Where I felt clarity so required, I replaced the English translation of the divine name (generally rendered "the LORD") with "Yahweh."

[3] Brevard Childs, *The Book of Exodus: A Critical, Theological Commentary* (Philadelphia: Westminster Press, 1974), 567.

[4] John I. Durham, *Exodus*, Word Biblical Commentary (Waco, TX: Word Books, 1987), 429.

[5] Childs, *Exodus*, 567.

[6] Peter Enns, *Exodus*, The NIV Application Commentary (Grand Rapids: Zondervan, 2000), 571.

[7] Walter C. Kaiser, Jr., "Exodus," in *The Expositor's Bible Commentary*, ed.

Frank E. Gaebelein (Grand Rapids: Zondervan, 1990), 278.

[8] Walter Brueggemann, "The Book of Exodus," in *The New Interpreter's Bible*, ed. Leander E. Keck (Nashville: Abingdon Press, 1994), 931.

[9] Durham, 429.

[10] Donald E. Gowan, *Theology in Exodus: Biblical Theology in the Form of a Commentary* (Louisville, Kentucky: Westminster John Knox Press, 1994), 221.

[11] Enns, 571.

[12] Terence E. Fretheim, *Exodus*, Interpretation (Louisville: John Knox Press, 1991), 283.

[13] Ibid., 284.

[14] Childs, *Exodus*, 567.

[15] Enns, 571-72.

[16] Gowen, 222.

[17] Ibid., 223.

[18] Ibid.

[19] Fretheim, *Exodus*, 283. The psalmist later recounts this episode, noting that Yahweh "would [have] destroy[ed] them—had not Moses, his chosen one, stood in the breach before him to keep his wrath from destroying them" (Ps 106:23).

[20] Gowan, 223.

[21] Childs, *Exodus*, 568.

[22] Fretheim, *Exodus*, 283-84. Yahweh's requiring the consent of Moses, however, does not minimize the seriousness of the threat or the intensity with which Moses sought to save the people from Yahweh's wrath. Indeed, Deuteronomy 9:25 tells of Moses' lying prostrate before Yahweh for forty days and forty nights interceding on behalf of the people (Childs, *Exodus*, 568). Some may argue that Yahweh is testing Moses to see if he would simply accept Yahweh's new promise and disregard his role as mediator for the people. There is no support for this in the narrative, however, which paints Yahweh's response to Moses' intercession as a genuine change of heart (Fretheim, *Exodus*, 284). In addition, as an argument against open theism, this position accomplishes little, as the need to test Moses would introduce a level of uncertainty into God's knowledge of the future.

[23] Durham, 429. Yahweh's frustration is easily understandable in light of the surrounding context. During the Sinai experience beginning in chapter 19, Yahweh gives the Israelites his laws, finishing his speech to the people with a warning not to serve other gods. To this the people respond, "We will do everything Yahweh has said; we will obey" (24:3). Yet, the very next recorded statement of the people is "Come, make us gods who will go before us. As for this fellow Moses who brought us up out of Egypt, we don't know what has happened to him." The people were quick to turn away in-

deed (J. Clinton McCann, Jr., "Exodus 32:1-14," *Interpretation* 44.3 (Jul 1990): 227).

[24] McCann, 283.

[25] Fretheim, *Exodus*, 283.

[26] Moses is thereby assuming Yahweh to be a God who takes reason and logic into account when making decisions (Fretheim, *Exodus*, 285).

[27] Enns, 572.

[28] Durham, 429.

[29] Gowan, 224.

[30] Ibid.

[31] Durham, 429.

[32] Brueggemann, 932.

[33] Durham, 429.

[34] Fretheim, *Exodus*, 285.

[35] Enns, 572.

[36] Durham, 429.

[37] Fretheim, *Exodus*, 285-86. Although Yahweh could have remained true to his covenant with Abraham through Moses—since Moses was a descendant of Abraham—it would have been like starting with a new Abraham, which the narrative never portrays as a desirable option (Fretheim, *Exodus*, 286).

[38] Ibid., 286.

[39] Ibid. During his appeal, Moses "sought the favor of Yahweh his God." The word translated "sought" in the NIV appears elsewhere in Scripture to describe sickness or affliction (e.g., Gen 48:1; Deut 29:22). In Judges 16:17, for example, when Samson tells Delilah the secret of his strength, he uses the word to say, "If my head were shaved, my strength would leave me, and I would *become as weak* as any other man" (emphasis added). The word carries with it connotations of humility. Though Yahweh takes Moses' arguments very seriously, Moses seeks Yahweh's favor by humbling himself. Yahweh's sovereignty in determining these matters is never in doubt.

[40] These passages never indicate that God repents of sin, as if any of God's actions were inappropriate or unjust. Instead, they teach that God repents of evil, that is, judgment. "Hence God's repenting of evil has reference to a decision for judgment" (Ibid., 286).

[41] Durham, 429.

[42] See Childs, *Exodus*, 568.

[43] Durham, 429.

[44] Childs, *Exodus*, 568.

[45] Perhaps it could be argued that Yahweh delayed judgment in order to save the lives of future generations of Israelites. This would not, however, negate his repentance in the sense that he had originally intended to com-

pletely annihilate the nation, thereby assuring the nonexistence of future generations. Saving their lives still represents a reversal in the divine plan.

[46] Notice that God changes his mind, not on his own in divine isolation, but *in response* to the people of Nineveh. Scripture does not teach that God is like a man changing his mind, wavering back and forth in an indecisive uncertainty. God's repentance results only from the effects of his genuine relationship with humanity.

[47] "Relents" in Jonah 4:2 is the same Hebrew word used in other passages of divine repentance described above.

[48] Clement was bishop of Rome in the late first century, making him the fourth pope according to Roman Catholic tradition. It is possible that *1 Clement*, which is traditionally ascribed to him, dates earlier than some New Testament material.

[49] Of course, Calvinists escape this by arguing that God decided whom he would save and whom he would damn (or allow to be damned) before the foundations of the earth.

[50] J. Daniel Hays, "Anthropomorphism, Revelation, and the Nature of God in the Old Testament," a paper utilized for THEO 4133 Old Testament Theology, Ouachita Baptist University, May 2003, rev. September 2, 2004, 1.

[51] Besides attesting to divine repentance, this passage also demonstrates Yahweh's perception of the future in terms of possibilities. Notice Yahweh tells Moses that he *might* destroy the people along the way should he accompany them. Yahweh expresses this as one possible future, though not the only one, as the rest of the Pentateuch demonstrates.

[52] See Boyd, *God of the Possible*, 70.

[53] Terence Fretheim offers a compelling case for an open model of God through his tracing of various motifs throughout the Old Testament in the fourth chapter of his *The Suffering of God* (Philadelphia: Fortress Press, 1984). What follows under the subsequent subheadings, which are also drawn from chapter four of *The Suffering of God*, is, except where otherwise noted, a summary of Fretheim's compelling work on the matter. For a more thorough discussion of these motifs see Fretheim, *Suffering*, 45-59.

[54] Fretheim, *Suffering*, 45-46.
[55] Ibid., 46.
[56] Boyd, *God of the Possible*, 70.
[57] Fretheim, *Suffering*, 47.
[58] Ibid.
[59] Ibid., 48-49.
[60] See Ibid.
[61] Boyd, *God of the Possible*, 67-68.
[62] Ibid., 69.

[63] Ibid., 66-67.

[64] Ibid., 52.

[65] Ibid.

[66] Abraham Joshua Heschel, *A Passion for Truth* (New York: Farrar, Straus & Giroux, 1973), 265, 269, quoted in Philip Yancey, *Prayer: Does It Make Any Difference?* (Grand Rapids: Zondervan, 2006), 96.

[67] Fretheim, *Suffering*, 55.

[68] Ibid., 56. For a more thorough discussion of the motif of the divine question, see Fretheim, *Suffering*, 53-59.

[69] John Calvin, *Institutes of the Christian Religion*, ed. John T. McNeill (Philadelphia: Westminster, 1960), 1.31.1, quoted in John Sanders, *The God Who Risks: A Theology of Providence* (Downers Grove, Illinois: InterVarsity Press, 1998), 33.

[70] Gregory A. Boyd, *Satan and the Problem of Evil: Constructing a Trinitarian Warfare Theodicy* (Downers Grove, Illinois: InterVarsity Press, 2001), 98.

[71] Robert B. Chisholm, Jr., "Does God 'Change His Mind?'" *Bibliotheca Sacra* 152 (Oct-Dec 1995): 387.

[72] Sanders, *God Who Risks*, 22.

[73] Thomas Aquinas, *Summa Theologica*, ed. Anton C. Pegis, 2 vols. (New York: Random House, 1945), 1. QQ13. A1, quoted in Sanders, *God Who Risks*, 23.

[74] Sanders, *God Who Risks*, 23.

[75] Hillary of Poitiers, *On the Trinity* 4.14, in *Nicene and Post-Nicene Fathers*, ed. Philip Schaff, 2nd series (Grand Rapids: Eerdmans, 1983), 9:75, quoted in Sanders, *God Who Risks*, 23. Calvin himself argued that God and God alone bears the responsibility of defining himself, which is exactly what God does in Scripture. "God cannot reveal himself to us in any other way than by a comparison with things we know" (John Calvin, *The Commentaries of John Calvin on the Old Testament* (Edinburgh: Calvin Translation Society, 1843-1848), 15:223 and Calvin, *Institutes*, 1.13.21, both quoted in Sanders, *God Who Risks*, 24). Unfortunately, Calvin fails to consistently apply this truth to his own hermeneutics.

[76] For the sake of argument, I use the word "literal" as it is often used in this debate, meaning not metaphorical. As N. T. Wright points out throughout his various writings, particularly his *Christian Origins and the Question of God* series, this is often not the most helpful way to define the term. Exploring the subject further, however, is beyond the scope of this book, and so for the sake of consistency, I assume the definition often assumed within this debate.

[77] Even if God only appears to change his mind or experience uncertainty, he clearly reveals himself as a God who does. If believers deny that God

can change his mind or experience uncertainty because of the affirmation that God is "unqualifiedly infinite, unlimited and immovable," then believers deny God's self-revelation in Scripture based upon philosophical presuppositions. Besides, such descriptions of God are meaningless, since such a God cannot be known *a priori* (Sanders, *God Who Risks*, 23). Christians must accept God's teachings about himself and not try to cram him into the Greco-Roman philosophical assumption that a perfect deity must be unchanging in every aspect (Gregory A. Boyd, *Is God to Blame: Moving Beyond Pat Answers to the Problem of Evil* (Downers Grove, Illinois: InterVarsity Press, 2003), 42-43).

[78] Boyd, *Satan*, 99.

[79] See Hays, 8-9.

[80] Fretheim, *Suffering*, 7. For a thorough discussion of the use of metaphors in Scripture, see Fretheim, *Suffering*, ch. 1.

[81] Eli C. Minkoff and Pamela J. Baker, *Biology Today: An Issues Approach*, 3rd ed (New York: Garland Publishing, 2004), 30.

[82] I am indebted to Dr. J. Daniel Hays, who shared with me a story about a blind student of his who frequently used this very expression.

[83] Boyd, *Satan*, 99. See also Sanders, *God Who Risks*, 66-75.

[84] Boyd, *God of the Possible*, 77.

[85] Calvin, *Institutes*, 1.17.13, 227, quoted in Boyd, *Satan*, 98.

[86] Boyd, *Satan*, 98-99.

[87] Ibid.

[88] Ibid.

[89] Boyd, *God of the Possible*, 77.

[90] While taking histories in Scripture to be normative for beliefs and values can be dangerous, understanding the purposes of the author and the theology driving the historical account does provide valuable and, according to the evangelical perspective, infallible theological truths. God cannot act contrary to his nature, and so accounts of God's acts in history must be consistent with that nature. Therefore, histories are invaluable in understanding the divine nature.

[91] Ibid., 77-78.

[92] Ibid.

[93] Boyd, *Satan*, 98.

[94] Kent Sparks, "The Sun Also Rises: Accommodation in Inscripturation in Interpretation," in *Evangelicals and Scripture: Tradition, Authority, and Hermeneutics*, ed. V. Bacote, L. Miguélez and D. Okholm (Downers Grove, Illinois: InterVarsity Press, 2004), 127, quoted in Hays, 4-5.

[95] Sanders, *God Who Risks*, 295.

[96] Hays, 8.

[97] N. T. Wright, "The Laing Lecture 1989, and the Griffith Thomas Lec-

ture 1989."

[98] Hays, 1.

[99] God's removing the kingship from Saul makes most sense if God did not know with certainty what Saul would do with the kingship when he bestowed it upon him. (Terence E. Fretheim, "Divine Foreknowledge, Divine Constancy, and the Rejection of Saul's Kingship," *Catholic Biblical Quarterly* (Oct 1985): 595).

[100] Norman L. Geisler, *Creating God in the Image of Man? The New Open View of God—Neotheism's Dangerous Drift* (Minneapolis: Bethany House, 1997), 78, 89, 90, 108, quoted in Sanders, *God Who Risks*, 67.

[101] Bruce Ware, "An Evangelical Reformulation of the Doctrine of the Immutability of God," *Journal of the Evangelical Theological Society* 29, no. 4 (1986): 442.

[102] Boyd, *God of the Possible*, 79-80.

[103] Ibid., 80; so also Sanders, *God Who Risks*, 69.

[104] Fretheim, *Suffering*, 51.

[105] Boyd, *God of the Possible*, 80; so also Sanders, *God Who Risks*, 69.

[106] Sanders, *God Who Risks*, 70.

[107] Boyd, *God of the Possible*, 80.

[108] Ibid., 80-81.

[109] Ibid., 81.

[110] Ibid.

[111] Fretheim, *Suffering*, 57.

[112] Boyd, *God of the Possible*, 41.

[113] Ibid.

[114] Fretheim, *Suffering*, 57.

[115] William Hasker, "A Philosophical Perspective," in *The Openness of God* (Downers Grove, Illinois: InterVarsity Press, 1994), 153.

[116] Boyd, *Satan*, 94.

[117] Doubts concerning the dating of 1 Kings raises the question, Did the prophet actually prophesy the name Josiah, or did the redactor provide the name in order to point to Josiah's reforms—with which the readers would have been familiar—as the fulfillment of this prophecy? Scribal interpolation is a well-understood issue that does not in itself threaten the evangelical doctrine of the infallibility or inerrancy of Scripture.

[118] See Fretheim, *Suffering of God*, ch. 4. Some may argue that God expresses a desire that the people will repent, even though he knows they will not. This, however, fails to make sense of—and seems to contradict—the divine perhaps motif previously discussed.

[119] Boyd, *God of the Possible*, 71-72.

[120] Ibid., 72-73.

[121] Sanders, *God Who Risks*, 295.

[122] Boyd, *God of the Possible*, 171.
[123] Ibid.
[124] Ibid, 36; Joel B. Green, *The Gospel of Luke*, The New International Commentary on the New Testament (Grand Rapids: Eerdmans, 1997), 773.
[125] Green, 772-73.
[126] Boyd, *God of the Possible*, 47.
[127] Ibid., 46-47.
[128] Arminain theologians avoid this conclusion by arguing that God predestines the elect based on his foreknowledge of their acceptance of the gospel according to their own free will. As I will discuss in next chapter, however, this position is logically incoherent.
[129] N. T. Wright, *The New Testament and the People of God* (Minneapolis: Fortress Press, 1992), 259-62, 264.
[130] Ibid., 264.
[131] James D. G. Dunn, *The Theology of Paul the Apostle* (Grand Rapids: Eerdmans, 1998), 526.
[132] Brevard S. Childs, *Old Testament Theology in a Canonical Context* (Philadelphia: Fortress Press, 1985), 92. "Conversely, the nations are to bear testimony that the divine 'law shall go forth out of Zion and the Word of God from Jerusalem' (Isa 2:3.) The nations confess: 'God is with you only, and there is no god beside him' (Isa 45:14)."
[133] Childs, *Old Testament Theology*, 103-02. This responsibility of Israel is most clearly reflected in the book of Jonah.
[134] Cited by Wright, *People of God*, 267.
[135] C. Marvin Pate, J. Scott Duvall, J. Daniel Hays, E. Randolph Richards, W. Dennis Tucker, Jr., and Preben Vang, *The Story of Israel: A Biblical Theology* (Downers Grove, Illinois: InterVarsity Press, 2004), 207.
[136] Childs, *Old Testament*, 92.
[137] See Pate and others, *Israel*, 206-31.
[138] Ibid., 207-08.
[139] C. Marvin Pate, *The Reverse of the Curse* (Tübingen: Mohr Siebeck, 2000), 153.
[140] Sanders, *God Who Risks*, 121.
[141] Ibid., 119. Sanders argues that God intended to fulfill his promise to Abraham through Israel's coming to faith in Christ. The Gentiles would then be united with believing Israel, not through the law, but through Christ (Sanders, *God Who Risks*, 117-09).
[142] Pate, *Curse*, 259-60; see also Pate and others, *Israel*, 211-12.
[143] Douglas Moo, *The Epistle to the Romans*, The New International Commentary on the New Testament (Grand Rapids: Eerdmans, 1996), 701.
[144] Pate, *Curse*, 224-05.
[145] Pate and others, *Israel*, 211-12.

[146] Ibid.

[147] James D. G. Dunn, *Romans 9-16*, Word Biblical Commentary (New York: T & T Clark International, 1979), 695.

[148] Pate and others, *Israel*, 219.

[149] Dunn, *Romans*, 696.

[150] Pate and others, *Israel*, 228.

[151] Sanders, *God Who Risks*, 121. Badges of the covenant members would include such Jewish rites as circumcision, observance of the Sabbath, and adherence to dietary laws.

[152] Boyd, *Is God to Blame?*, 172.

[153] Pate, *Curse*, 259-60.

[154] Dunn, *Romans*, 693.

[155] Pate and others, *Israel*, 230.

[156] Dunn, *Theology*, 504.

[157] Jack W. Cottrell, "The Nature of Divine Sovereignty," in *The Grace of God and the Will of Man*, ed. Clark H. Pinnock (Minneapolis: Bethany House, 1995), 114.

[158] Sanders, *God Who Risks*, 121.

[159] Ibid.

[160] W. S. Campbell, "Israel," in *The Dictionary of Paul and His Letters*, ed. Gerald F. Hawthorne and Ralph Martin (Downers Grove, Illinois: InterVarsity Press, 1993): 443.

[161] Ibid.

[162] Dunn, *Theology*, 502. See Dunn, *Theology*, 340-46 for a thorough discussion on God's righteousness as it relates to his covenant faithfulness.

[163] Campbell, 443.

[164] Ibid. This is not to say that God will save every individual Israelite whether they want him to save them or not. Rather, it means that despite Israel's continued sin, God remains committed to their corporate identity.

[165] Dunn, *Theology*, 525; so also George Eldon Ladd, *A Theology of the New Testament* (Grand Rapids: Eerdmans, 1974), 583.

[166] Ibid., 508.

[167] Ibid.

[168] H. J. Kraus, *The People of God in the Old Testament* (New York: Association Press, 1958), 89, quoted in Ladd, 583.

[169] Dunn, *Theology*, 525; so also Campbell, 441.

[170] Campbell, 441.

[171] Dunn, *Theology*, 525.

[172] Moo, 715.

[173] C. E. B. Cranfield, *Romans 9-16*, International Critical Commentary (New York: T & T Clark International, 1979), 574; so also Thomas R. Schreiner, *Romans*, Baker Exegetical Commentary on the New Testament

(Grand Rapids: Baker Academics, 1988), 613.

[174] Moo, 714; so also Dunn, 678, 680; Cranfield, 573; Schreiner, 613. This mystery may have been revealed to Paul through study of the Old Testament in light of the Gospel, though a special revelation is likely. See Dunn, 678; Cranfield, 573.

[175] John R. W. Stott, *The Message of Romans*, The Bible Speaks Today (Downers Grove, Illinois: InterVarsity Press, 1994), 302.

[176] Moo, 713; so also Cranfield, 574; Schreiner, 613, 621.

[177] Stott, 302.

[178] Dunn, *Theology*, 501.

[179] Moo, 713; so also Campbell 444-45.

[180] Dunn, *Theology*, 511.

[181] Moo, 730; so also Stott, 306; Dunn, 693; Campbell, 442.

[182] Cranfield, 580; so also Schreiner, 625.

[183] Ibid., 444; so also Ladd, 582-83.

[184] Moo, 731; so also Dunn, 685; Cranfield, 581; Schreiner, 626-27; Dunn, 694; Campbell, 442. This stands against the "merits of the fathers" position which Paul would have probably found repugnant. See Cranfield, 580-81; Schreiner, 626-27.

[185] Schreiner, 626.

[186] G. Baum, *Is the New Testament Anti-Semitic?* (Glen Rock, N.J.: Paulist, 1965), 294, quoted in Charles M. Horne, "The Meaning of the Phrase 'And Thus All Israel Will Be Saved' (Romans 11:26)," *Journal of the Evangelical Theological Society* 21 (Dec 1978): 329.

[187] Ladd, 583.

[188] Richard A. Batey, "So All Israel Will Be Saved: An Interpretation of Romans 11:25-32," *Interpretation* 20 (April 1966): 222.

[189] Moo, 712; so also Dunn, *Romans*, 680.

[190] Sanders, *God Who Risks*, 121. The Hebrew word used to describe the hardening of Pharaoh's heart in Exodus 7:2 literally means, "to be hard." The root word is used elsewhere when referring to stiff-necked people (Ex 32:9, 33:3-5, 34:9, Ezek 2:4, 3:7). In Exodus 7:2, the narrative stresses *Pharaoh's* resolve against Yahweh, by refusing to obey and instead oppressing the people all the more. Pharaoh is still accountable for his actions, for it is not impossible for one with a hardened heart to be persuaded by outside events. For example, Yahweh hardens the hearts of Pharaoh's servants (Ex 10:1), yet they see the negative impact of divine judgment on Egypt and urge Pharaoh to change his ways (10:7) (Fretheim, 96-98). Israel's hardening should be understood similarly.

[191] Dunn, *Romans*, 696; so also Cranfield, 587; Dunn, *Theology*, 513.

[192] Boyd, *Satan*, 82.

[193] Moo, 713.

[194] Stott, 303; so also Moo, 717.
[195] Moo, 717.
[196] Dunn, *Romans*, 680; so also Moo, 717.
[197] See Ibid., 671.
[198] Ibid.
[199] Ibid.
[200] Moo, 724.
[201] Schreiner, 629.
[202] Stott, 307.
[203] Ibid.
[204] Dunn, *Romans*, 668.
[205] Horne, 330.
[206] Moo, 720-21.
[207] Stott, 303.
[208] Moo, 721.
[209] Ibid., 722; so also Dunn, *Romans*, 681. A variation of this is the belief that "all Israel" means the Jewish remnants from every single generations (cf. Horne, 333-34) . This, however, is very unlikely for reasons cited above (Schreiner, 616-17).

[210] John Murray, *The Epistle to the Romans*, Volume 2, The New International Commentary on the New Testament (Grand Rapids: Eerdmans, 1968), 96, quoted in Stott, 303.

[211] Dunn, *Romans*, 681; so also Campbell, 444-45; Cranfield, 576-77; Schreiner, 615; Stott, 303; Moo, 722; Ladd, 584. There is no reason to take "all Israel will be saved" as a declaration of universal salvation for Jews. Since the same word is used for the fullness of Israel and the fullness of the Gentiles, an affirmation of universal Jewish salvation would, in effect, be an affirmation of universalism. Either conclusion contradicts Paul's message throughout the book of Romans that all have sinned and can only be saved by faith in Christ—though the issue of universalism and the debate surrounding its teachings within the early church are beyond the scope of this book.

[212] F. F. Bruce, *The Letter of Paul to the Romans*, The Tyndale New Testament Commentaries (InterVarsity Press and Eerdmans, 1963): 209, quoted in Stott, 303.

[213] Campbell, 444.
[214] Dunn, *Theology*, 508-11.
[215] Ibid.
[216] Ibid.
[217] Ibid.
[218] Ibid.
[219] Ibid.

[220] Moo, 713, 723. Paul's argument that "all Israel will be saved" does not contradict his argument in Romans 9 that only a remnant of Israel will inherit salvation because "all Israel" does not mean all Israel throughout history, but only all Israel in the eschaton. The saving of all of Israel at the end of time is still only a remnant of Israel when compared to all of Israel throughout history (Schreiner, 621-22).

[221] Campbell, 445.

[222] Sanders, *God Who Risks*, 122-23.

[223] Dunn, *Romans*, 681.

[224] Ibid., 691; so also Moo, 722.

[225] Ibid., 695.

[226] Cranfield, 585.

[227] Campbell, 445.

[228] Dunn, *Romans*, 695.

[229] Ibid., 658; see also Campbell, 445.

[230] Campbell, 445.

[231] Dunn, *Theology*, 508.

[232] Ibid., 680.

[233] Ibid.; so also Moo, 724.

[234] Ibid., 527. Any discussion of Paul's understanding of Israel and eschatology must address 1 Thessalonians 2:14-16. That passage does not reject the possibility of Israel's salvation, nor does it contradict Romans 11. Notice that Paul is writing against his own nation and his own people. There is no gleeful invoking of judgment upon Israel, but only grief over her sins, reflected later as he pens Romans 9. Furthermore, Paul's harsh words are not directed against Jews in general—Paul is, after all, a Jew—but against those who have rejected the gospel. Paul's anger is against only those Jews involved in the named activities (Leon Morris, *The First and Second Epistles to the Thessalonians*, New International Commentary on the New Testament (Grand Rapids: Eerdmans, 1991), 83, 85).

3 PHILOSOPHY AND SYSTEMATICS

For the typical evangelical, steeped in traditional Reform-era theology, accepting open theism requires a tremendous philosophical and theological paradigm shift in thinking, for it is here that the differences between the open and traditional positions are the most pronounced. An evaluation of the philosophical and systematic implications of open theism is therefore necessary to determine what place it can claim within the realm of evangelical thought.

A Paradigm Shift

The exegetical and hermeneutical conclusions of open theology as outlined in the previous chapter demand a change in thinking about the nature of God, particularly in the traditional understandings of immutability, impassibility, and foreknowledge.

Divine Immutability

The doctrine of divine immutability has stood for centuries as a pillar of traditional theological thought with roots in Aristotle's Unmoved Mover and its Christian reformulation by Thomas Aquinas. The open model of God, however, with its affirmation of God's ability to change his mind and expand his knowledge as new truths come into existence, challenges this understanding of the divine nature.

To defend immutability, traditional theologians turn to philosophical arguments dating back to Plato. Their central contention lies with the relationship between change and perfection. According to Platonian philosophy, change must either be for better or for worse. God, being a perfect being, cannot change for the better, for one cannot improve on perfection, nor can he change for the worse, as that would negate his perfection. God, therefore, cannot change.[1] In support of this position, Augustine of Hippo wrote, "Whatever is changeable is not the most high God,"[2] and "that which truly is is that which unchangeably abides."[3]

The strength of this argument, however, is not as straightforward as it may seem. The Christian theologian runs into a serious problem Plato did not have to face: tension with the biblical witness. This understanding of God relies on philosophy to determine the nature of God over and against scriptural revelation. This is a case of traditional theologians and philosophers concluding that God is a perfect being, then determining for themselves what qualities perfection necessitates.[4]

"In this way God's nature is made to conform to our notions of what deity should be like and, if the Bible does not measure up to this standard in its speech about God, we invoke our own subjective criteria to correct it."[5] Undoubtedly, adherence to commonly accepted Christian orthodoxy necessitates acceptance of God's perfection. Faithfulness to Christian Scripture and a sound exegetical method, however, require that God himself, and not the pagan Plato, determines what perfection entails.

The second major problem with this argument is its basis in a false philosophical assumption that all change is for better or worse, not allowing for quality-neutral change. Consider a perfectly operational wristwatch. The time is constantly changing on the watch, but that change is neither for better or worse. Rather, the change itself is a sign that the watch is perfectly operational. Indeed, no one would consider an immutable watch perfect.[6] Change demonstrates that it is behaving properly.

Consider also the change of seasons. If the seasons ceased to change the results would be devastating. These changes are not for better or worse but rather are changes that are "consistent with and/or required by a constant state of excellence."[7]

In reality, open theists and traditionalists both maintain divine immutability. The two schools of thought simply define the term differently. Consider the examples above. In a sense, both the seasons and the watch are immutable. Spring always follows winter, summer always follows spring, and one o'clock always precedes two o'clock. The changing of seasons is part of the unchanging nature of the seasonal cycle, and the constant time change on the watch corresponds to the unchanging—though relative—reality of the passage of time.

Open theists define divine immutability in this sense. God "does change in his actions and emotions to men when given proper grounds for doing so…he does not change in his basic integrity of character."[8] His character, love, and nature are immutable. God is perfect, and he is unchanging in his perfection.

Part of his unchanging perfection, however, is his ability to relate in a very personal way to his creation, changing and adapting his plans to accommodate free agents, changing his mind in response to their prayers, and allowing them to contribute to the formation of the future so that his knowledge changes to correspond perfectly to changes in reality. God's ability to adapt in response to his people is a sign of his loving, dynamic relationship with his creation, a further testament to his perfection and a reflection of his immutable nature.

Just because God does not change does not mean that there can be no change with God. What is admirable about a God who resides in a static existence with no dynamic interaction with anyone outside himself? Indeed, according to the biblical witness, immutability in this sense is a hindrance to and not an attribute of divine perfection.

Of course, the traditional understanding of divine immutability suffers its harshest blow in Christian theology at the hand of the incarnation. When infinite God became finite man in the form of Jesus Christ, he underwent a dramatic change, dismissing outright the Platonic understanding of divine immutability. Efforts to preserve immutability in the face of the incarnation, such as by making distinctions between the divine and human natures of Christ, water down the significance of the incarnation—and indeed flirt with the teachings of fourth and fifth century heresies. It seems more helpful simply to redefine immutability in light of the biblical witness.

Divine Impassibility

Impassibility forms another foundational pillar in classical theological thought with roots in the writings of Aristole. Divine impassibility is "the claim that God's perfection requires that God be completely self-contained, not influenced or conditioned in any way by creatures, and in particular incapable of any suffering, distress or negative emotions of any kind."[9]

In accordance with this doctrine, Anselm once prayed, "Thou art both compassionate, because thou dost save the wretched, and spare those who sin against thee; and not compassionate, because thou are affected by no sympathy for wretchedness." In other words, God behaves as one would expect a compassionate being to behave, but an impassible nature is incapable of compassion.[10]

Open theists adamantly deny the validity of divine impassibility, for at the heart of open theology is the strong affirmation that God maintains a personal, give-and-take relationship with his creation. This requires a God genuinely affected by others. Impassibility, like immutability, relies on pre-Christian pagan philosophical thought at the expense of the biblical witness, for a God who can genuinely respond to his creation—by changing his mind for example—cannot be impassible. Additionally, impassibility, like immutability, is dealt a huge blow by the incarnation.

The Gospel accounts clearly describe Jesus' experiencing the full range of human emotions and suffering during his time on earth. Since orthodox Christian theology teaches that Jesus was the full revelation of God, reason necessitates that if Jesus were not impassible, then God is not impassible or at least divinity does not necessitate impassibility, as Aristotelian thought teaches. If divinity does not necessitate impassibility, then efforts to preserve it are unnecessary.

Origen recognized this very issue and, in an effort to preserve his philosophical presuppositions, concluded that only the human side of Jesus suffered. The divine nature of Christ remained totally untouched by the incarnation.[11] The First Council of Nicea in 325 and the Council of Ephesus in 431 taught that Jesus was both completely God and completely man and that his divine and human natures were united. This is the only accepted position within orthodox Christianity.[12]

If this is accepted, then there was no aspect of Christ that was not both divine and human, and so no clear dichotomy between his divine and human nature exists, making the two inseparable.[13] One cannot be isolated from the other. Therefore to claim that Christ's divine nature was unaffected by that which affected his human nature is philosophically incoherent and comes dangerously close to falling into the Nestorian heresy. If Christ's human nature suffered, then his divine nature suffered as well.

The Arians understood that Origen's claim was ludicrous, and so denied the total divinity of Christ in order, among other things, to preserve their own similar philosophical presuppositions regarding the divine nature.[14] The adamant refusal of open theists to accept divine impassibility brings their school of thought more in line with the revelation of Scripture and therefore more, not less, in line with the presuppositions of evangelical theology.

The traditional impassible model of God is simply incompatible with the God of Scripture. Scripture does not present an impassible God, but a God profoundly affected by his creation, a God who mourns the adulterous idolatry of his people in the Old Testament, and a God who endures a hellish death in the New Testament. Indeed, the God who restrained his omnipotence on the cross continues to restrain it in his relationship with us.

Scripture depicts a God who is genuinely affected by a world that he loves deeply. He is a God who is willing to endure extraordinary suffering and pain to maintain his bond with a sinful humanity. Indeed, "[b]ecause this condescending God fully relates to sinful creatures with integrity, and with the deepest possible love, God cannot but suffer, and in manifold ways."[15] Nowhere is this more clear than in the depiction of Christ crucified.

Furthermore, formulating doctrines of God *a priori*, apart from Scripture, is counterproductive. If God is impassible, then his character stands in contradiction with his revelation of himself in Scripture. The God in Scripture is not an impassible God, but a relational one. Evangelicals, therefore, are obligated to accept him as such without attempting to circumvent the divine revelation to find impassibility. Indeed, "the one who enters into relationship with the world remains in the depth of his existence ultimately mysterious and beyond our ability to gain access through our innate ability to know."[16]

Divine Foreknowledge

Impassibility and immutability are not, however, the source of greatest controversy in this debate. Openness is so unsettling to classical systematicians because it threatens a foundational presupposition of traditional theology: exhaustive divine foreknowledge.

Philo argued that, since God foreknows all things that will ever transpire, certain actions of God as described in Scripture, such as divine repentance, are genuinely impossible.[17] Indeed, a God capable of repentance, regret, surprise, and "if" and "might" statements simultaneously possessing exhaustive foreknowledge of all future events, including his own actions, seems logically incoherent.

Some, such as Tertullian, have chosen to accept these seemingly contradictory points.[18] After all, only the "arrogant and the dogmatic find paradox hard to accept."[19] To the open theists, however, this is not a matter of paradox, comparable to Christ's ability to be simultaneously fully God and fully man, but a matter of logical contradiction. To simultaneously possess foreknowledge and be uncertain about future events is a contradiction in terms, similar to a square circle. In light of the biblical witness and in search of a more coherent system of theological thought, open theology has challenged the traditional understanding of God's foreknowledge and redefined it according to the biblical testimony.

(i) Denying omniscience?

Open theists often receive their most intense criticism over the doctrine of divine omniscience. Many critics of open theism charge that by denying God's foreknowledge of all future events, open theists deny God's omniscience. This, however, is an unfounded assertion. "Open theists affirm God's omniscience as emphatically as anybody does. The issue is not whether God's knowledge is perfect. It is. The issue is about the nature of the reality that God perfectly knows."[20] That is to say, the issue is not what God does or does not know; rather, the issue is what exists to be known.[21]

The emotionally charged language of divine capability has clouded the real area of disagreement between open and traditional theologians: the ontological reality of future events as they exist in the present. Open and traditional theologians both affirm that God knows everything that is, and nothing can exist outside the knowledge of God. The two schools of thought part ways, however, over exactly what exists to be known.[22]

Traditional theologians argue that the future is exhaustively settled, by either divine foreknowledge or divine determinism. In other words, the "'definiteness' of every event—the fact that it will occur *this* way and not any other way—eternally precedes the actual occurrence of the event."[23] Since God is omniscient and the future is a settled reality, then of course God possesses exhaustive foreknowledge of all future events.

Open theologians, however, contend with this understanding of the future. To them, the future consists of unsettled possibilities. Since God knows all of reality perfectly and Scripture seems to portray God as facing a partially open future, the future must indeed be partially open. Open theists argue that the future is a realm of possibilities—except where an omnipotent God has chosen to remove possibilities in favor of a settled reality or where present and past circumstances make future events inevitable—and God knows it as such. If God does not know for certain future free actions, for example, it is only because those future free actions do not yet exist to be known.

To the open theist, claiming God doesn't know the future is the same as claiming God doesn't know in what year George Washington landed on the moon. In this sense, to say that "God doesn't know" is not a statement of divine ignorance but simply a testament to a reality that does not exist to be known. In disagreeing about God's knowledge of future events, open and traditional theists "are disagreeing about the content of reality, not about the omniscience of God."[24] It is disingenuous to accuse open theists of denying God's omniscience simply because they have a different understanding about the existing contents of reality.[25]

Indeed, God exhaustively knows all contents of reality. When possibilities exist only as possibilities, God knows them as such, but when possibilities become knowable as actualities for the first time, at that moment, God knows them as such. In reality, divine foreknowledge is only a small aspect of a theological system based on understanding God's relationship with his creation.

The open theist's understanding of omniscience implies, of course, that God's knowledge expands and changes as events unfold, demonstrating a real change in God in response to a real change in his creation. The foundation of open theism is the understanding that "God's relationship to others in time and history is real and affects the very life of God."[26]

(ii) The futility of foreknowledge

The openness debate has sparked so much controversy because many see open theism as diminishing God's glory,[27] believing that a God who knows the future exhaustively is greater than a God who does not. Besides falling back into the trap of assuming that human beings are capable of determining what qualities perfection necessitates—exhaustive foreknowledge, for example—*a priori*, and then attributing those characteristics to God, this assumption is simply incorrect. In fact, by logical necessity, if God foreknew the future exhaustively, he would be unable to alter it.[28]

Consider David Basinger's example of Susan, a young woman who has received proposals of marriage from two different men and is seeking God's guidance as she tries to decide which proposal to accept.

> What sort of guidance might God choose to give her? God knows, of course, everything there is to know concerning the personality, temperament, physical condition and so on of each of the three persons involved, as well as their potential for future happiness under various conditions. He knows far more, then, than even the wisest and most skillful human marriage counselor. But what more would be added if we assume that God somehow "sees" the actual future? Suppose he looks into the future and sees Susan unhappily married to Tom. Could not God, on the basis of this, warn Susan that she had better accept Kenneth's offer instead? A moment's reflection will show this to be incoherent. What God knows is the *actual* future, the situation in which she actually is married to Tom. So it is nonsensical to suggest that God, knowing the actual future, could on the basis of this knowledge influence things so that this would *not* be the actual future, which would mean that God would not know Susan as being married to Tom...I trust the point is clear. In general, to assume that God does anything in the present *on the basis of* his knowledge of the actual future *which could have an effect on that future* immediately leads us into the philosophical morass of circular explanation and circular causation.[29]

Foreknowledge of future events does nothing to add to God's glory, but rather shows God—from the human perspective at least, which is the only perspective from which man can relate to him—helplessly anticipating all the horrors of world history from all eternity, or worse, predestining them. A God seeing the future in terms of possibilities, however, would be able to anticipate *possible* tragedies and intervene so that they don't become *actual* tragedies. This is the model of God suggested by openness, and it is a model compatible with the biblical witness.

(iii) Issues of time and timelessness

While the nature of time is beyond the scope of this book and indeed far beyond the scope of this field of study, some have attempted to use scientific understandings of time to argue in favor of traditional theism. I generally believe this type of approach to theological studies to be a mistake, conflating two separate areas of study that rarely intersect. Nevertheless, for the sake of these arguments, open theists must recognize scientific discoveries applicable to their philosophical model of time.

According to modern scientific theory, there was a time prior to the big bang when the entire universe was compacted into an infinitesimally small and infinitely dense state of existence. In this condition, all scientific laws were nonexistent, at least in the sense that modern science understands them. Any events that may have occurred "prior" to this time are insignificant for they would have no effect on present conditions because those events would not have any observable consequences. "One may say that time had a beginning at the big bang, in the sense that earlier times simply would not be defined."[30]

Of course, this opens up another controversial debate surrounding the interpretation of Genesis 1 in relation to modern science, which is well beyond the scope of this book. Suffice it to say that God could have created the universe through the big bang, or he could have created an expanding universe that only suggests a big bang. The point is simply that the universe's state of constant expansion "does not preclude a creator, but it does place limits on when he might have carried out his job!"[31] This is all simply to say that the human concept of time has no meaning prior to the existence of the universe.[32] God's existence prior to the creation of the universe therefore demands that time is not an eternally existent entity with God.

Clearly then, God is beyond the scope of, or "above," time. Since time and space are not completely separable concepts but rather exist in combination with one another to form one object referred to as space-time,[33] it stands to reason that time requires space and mass to exist, and temporal experience, as far as science can tell, applies only to that which is bound by space-time.[34] Therefore, God, as creator of the universe, is not bound by space-time and therefore must not experience time in the same way as human beings.

Einstein's general theory of relativity states that space and time both act upon and are acted upon by every occurrence in the universe because "when a body moves, or a force acts, it affects the curvature of space and time—and in turn the structure of space-time affects the way in which bodies move and forces act."[35] Consequently, to talk about the application or existence of space-time outside of the universe is meaningless.[36] To apply the human temporal experience to God is therefore problematic, unless

Christians accept God as existing only within realm of this universe. This may be acceptable to some forms of process thought, but not to open—or evangelical—theology. The argument that God experiences time just as humans do is not an accurate expression of open theism.

Contrary to popular belief, however, Einstein's theory of relativity did not demonstrate time to be an illusion. Rather, it disproved the Newtonian and Aristotelian concepts of time. Newton and Aristotle both believed that the time between two events could be measured unambiguously no matter who measured it. This understanding presents time as existing independent of space, an understanding which science has demonstrated to be untenable.[37]

> In other words, the theory of relativity put an end to the idea of absolute time! It appeared that each observer must have his own measure of time, as recorded by a clock carried by him, and that identical clocks carried by different observers would not necessarily agree.[38]

An individual's relative experience of time is affected by that individual's proximity to bodies of extreme mass and the speed at which the individual is traveling relative to the speed of light. For example, an individual living on a mountain will age faster relative to an individual living at the mountain's base,[39] and an individual traveling in a rocket ship near the speed of light will age significantly slower in relation to an individual who remains on earth. This seems to be paradoxical, but there is only a paradox if the concept of absolute time is presupposed. "In the theory of relativity, there is no unique absolute time, but instead each individual has his own personal measure of time that depends on where he is and how he is moving."[40]

According to Einstein's theory of relativity, human beings rely on light to carry information of reality to them because "if light cannot get from one region to another, no other information can."[41] Therefore, all human experience is delayed by the amount of time it takes light to transmit that information.

> For example, if the sun were to cease to shine at this very moment, it would not affect things on earth at the present time because they would be in the elsewhere of the event when the sun went out. We would know about it only after eight minutes, the time it takes light to reach us from the sun. Only then would events on earth lie in the future light cone of the event at which the sun went out. Similarly, we do not know what is happening at the moment farther away in the universe: the light that we see from distance galaxies left them millions of years ago, and in the case of the most distant object that we have seen, the light left some eight thousand million years ago.

Thus, when we look at the universe, we are seeing it as it was in the past.[42]

Even a common occurrence, such as a plate falling and shattering on the floor, becomes the present for an observer after the event actually happened relative to the plate because the observer must wait on the light reflected from the event to reach him. While the delay is incomprehensibly small, because of the finitude of the speed of light, there is a delay nonetheless.

It stands to reason, then, that God as an infinite being would not be dependent on light for his information, but would rather receive his information immediately. Indeed, returning to the example of distant galaxies, from our perspective, there are places in the universe where God—relative to us—sees "eight thousand million years" into the future. Considered in this light, God's knowledge of future events takes on a more complex and nuanced form.

God's "time" would therefore become absolute time. As an infinite being, God is able to reference one all-encompassing single point in time, an experience impossible for finite beings.

> This means that God's experience of others is not dependent on (relative to) the speed of light. He doesn't need to "wait" for information to arrive to him via the speed of light. He is "there" when the information originates. This means that for God—but for no one else—there *can* be an all-embracing "now" in which all the relative "nows" experienced by finite observers coincide.[43]

Science simply has nothing to say about how God experiences time or reality, but it does demonstrate human limitations in the experiencing of reality, suggesting that there are limitations in human experience that do not apply to God. This, however, does not negate sequential experience in the divine understanding of reality.

The issue is not time itself. The issue is experience. Open theists argue that God can exist outside of time—as we understand it—while still experiencing reality sequentially, rather than in some sort of eternal now. That being said, however, Christians should be careful how they apply the laws of science to their metaphysical understanding of God, since science has nothing to say about the supernatural realm. The scientific understanding of time as real (though relative) implies that it is real to humanity and so must be real to God insofar as he relates to humanity, but it says nothing about how God experiences reality in relation to himself.

In reality, the issue of God's existence outside of time, or his timelessness, is a product of theological and not scientific thought, most notably immutability (discussed above). From Parmenides to Plato to Plotinus, philosophical thought finds that perfection both metaphysically and valuationally necessitates permanence over change. God must therefore be changeless. This philosophical school of thought developed a strong doctrine of divine immutability which gave rise to the doctrine of divine timelessness, "since timelessness is the most effective way (and perhaps the only way) to rule out, once and for all, the possibility of change in God."[44]

The implications of this doctrine are immense, for if

> God were to experience two moments in time simultaneously, they would have to *be* simultaneous and thus the same moment! The view that God "sees" all moments in time simultaneously entails that all time is reduced to one moment. Our experience of temporal succession would then be an illusion. But if there is no real temporal succession there would be no *real* change either, and impetratory prayer for things to happen would become meaningless.[45]

There is simply no real scriptural basis to support the elaborate metaphysical paradigm developed to support divine timelessness.[46] Furthermore, it is simply too difficult to make sense of the doctrine. How can a timeless God residing in a static existence act in history, be aware of developing earthly circumstances and events, or respond to his people as he does throughout Scripture? How can he become a human being and experience life and reality as any other man? Moreover, its strong connection with the now widely dismissed doctrine of divine simplicity should give pause to those so quick to accept it as dogma.[47]

Evangelicalism is the branch of Christian thought most synonymous with a strong reliance on biblical authority. There seems to be no justification for making divine timelessness and whatever it entails a tenet of evangelical theology considering its lack of biblical support. At some point, Ockham's razor should come into play. If God reveals himself as a God experiencing events sequentially along with his people and interacting with his people within time, then God probably does experience reality sequentially. Developing elaborate and complex systematic and philosophical understandings of God's relationship to time without compelling biblical evidence to do so seems unnecessary when a much simpler explanation is so readily available. Developing complex arguments that straightforward biblical passages are simply phenomenological, not corresponding to an ontological reality, is hermeneutically and philosophically irresponsible.

For the sake of argument, however, what if, as an ontological reality, God is timeless in the traditional sense (experiencing reality in an eternal now)? What value is there in ascribing such a state to God being as such an expression of "reality" is meaningless to time-bound humanity? How can those who are time-bound begin to comprehend what it means to be outside of time? Perhaps God does not experience reality sequentially, but such an understanding of reality is beyond the grasp of those who do.

This is demonstrated even in the way proponents of divine timelessness describe the doctrine. Words and phrases such as "simultaneous experience," "eternal now," and "all moments" demonstrate the human inability to understand a timeless reality, since they are all temporal words. Proponents of divine timelessness are unable to explain their position without reverting to temporal vocabulary, rendering the tenability of the doctrine at the very least suspect.

How can human beings even attempt to grasp what the experience of static reality, apart from sequential experience, entails? How can human beings begin to understand what characterizes a non-sequential reality? "We can say that God is temporal because we can only speak of him as he exists in relation to us. Whatever eternity means, it cannot contradict the truth that God is temporally related to us as creatures."[48]

Through Scripture, God has revealed himself to humanity through a diminished, finite manifestation of himself, which can only be assumed to be as true to his infinite, undiminished self as humanity can possibly comprehend. God is, by nature, unknowable. He allows man to know him, however, by accommodating to his finitude and condescending to his level. Attempts to ascend to God's level in an effort to attain a knowledge of reality mankind cannot possibly grasp is counterproductive to theological pursuits. As Augustine stated in his own contemplation of God's relationship to time,

> If anyone finds your simultaneity beyond his understanding, it is not for me to explain it. Let him be content to say "What is this?" (Exod. 16:15). So too let him rejoice and delight in finding you who are beyond discovery rather than fail to find you by supposing you to be discoverable.[49]

Divine Sovereignty

(i) General Sovereignty

Opponents of open theism often argue that the open model of God undermines God's sovereignty, claiming that in order for God to be able to guarantee the achievement of his goals, everything must be under his complete control. Open theists counter that these objectors "limit God by asserting that God cannot decide which sort of sovereignty to practice."[50]

Open theists do in fact affirm God's absolute sovereignty over creation. Once again, however, they must redefine the term. They argue that there are two kinds of sovereignty: specific and general. Specific sovereignty maintains that there are absolutely no limitations, hindrances or insurmountable obstacles for God to achieve his will in every specific circumstance of the created order. God has *exhaustive* control over each situation.[51]

John Calvin argued that that there is no such thing as chance. Seemingly arbitrary events, such as one person's escaping a shipwreck while another drowns, or one mother's ability to feed her child while another's starves, are all meticulously planned by God. Every detail of every event transpires according to God's preordained plan. "For proponents of specific sovereignty there is no such thing as an accident or a genuine tragedy."[52]

Biblical accounts of God experiencing grief (Gen 6:6), changing his mind (Ex 32:14), resorting to plan B (Ex 4:14), responding to the actions of his people (Jer 18:6-10), experiencing surprise (Jer 3:7; 32:35), and depending on prayer (Jas 4:2), however, pose a serious threat to the scriptural viability of specific sovereignty. John Sanders writes,

> [T]hese sorts of things make no sense within the framework of specific sovereignty. If God always gets precisely what he desires in each and every situation, then it is incoherent to speak of God's being grieved about or responding to the human situation. How can God be grieved if precisely what God wanted to happened did happen?[53]

In addition, God's anger in response to sin is incoherent because "any sin is specifically what God wanted to come about."[54]

Ironically, even Augustine recognized this point when he wrote, "Alas for the sins of humanity! (Isa. 1:4) Man it is who says this and you have pity on him, because you made him and did not make sin in him."[55] Furthermore, the reality of this world stands in direct contradiction to Christ's prayer for Christian unity and mutual love. If reality corresponds to the will of God, then Christ seems to be at odds with the Father, undermining the orthodox understanding of Christ as the full revelation of God.[56]

General sovereignty, however, "maintains that God has sovereignly established a type of world in which God sets up general structures of an overall framework for meaning and allows the creatures significant input into exactly how things will turn out."[57] In this model, God, while maintaining the freedom to micromanage events should he see fit, refrains from exercising exhaustive control over everything that may transpire on earth. Consequently, there are events that occur on account of human decisions and chance that are not preordained by God.[58] This is not to say that God is incapable of practicing specific sovereignty, only that he chooses not to do so. God's restraining his omnipotence does not imply that he does not posses it.[59]

Omnipotence is limited by love; but there is no imperfection about that. The ultimate fact remains that God, the ground of omnipotent love, cannot be destroyed or corrupted, but it is essential to his being love that he can be changed and affected by what his own power permits to be.[60]

To the open theist, the difference between specific and general sovereignty is the difference between a God who reduces the divine-human relationship to an impersonal level through manipulation and coercion and a personal God who allows for genuine give-and-take in his relationship with humanity. "It requires tremendous wisdom, patience, love, faithfulness and resourcefulness to work with a world of independent beings. A God of sheer omnipotence can run a world of exhaustively controlled beings. But what is magnificent about that?"[61]

God's sovereignty ensures that he is never caught off guard or at a loss in new situations, but he has to respond to events as they happen and deal with new realities as they come into existence without knowing with absolute certainty what will happen beforehand.[62] The open model may seem to diminish God's sovereignty, but "the sovereignty that reigns unchallenged is not as absolute as the sovereignty that accepts risk."[63]

God in his sovereignty has chosen to create a world that allows other factors, besides himself, to contribute to the transpiring of events, including the decisions of free agents, circumstances, and chance. He can, by his wisdom and sheer omnipotence, guarantee that his overarching plans for creation will ultimately be fulfilled. "God has not given everything over to us. God is the one who established the conditions, and his overarching purposes cannot be thwarted. Whatever ability we have to thwart God's individual purposes is given us by God."[64]

> God's not knowing what cannot be known, namely, the future decisions of self-determining beings, does not detract from God's maximal knowledge or cause him to be either ignorant or misled. God's control, even of the unforeseen future, is not limited by his lack of knowledge. It is guaranteed by his omnipotence, and this is not threatened by the nonexistence of the future.[65]

Upon reflection, a God who is able to bring about his purposes without controlling every aspect of reality seems more powerful and more truly sovereign than a God who must meticulously control every detail of every event. One proponent of specific sovereignty demonstrates this point when writing, "If there is one single molecule in this universe running around loose, totally free of God's sovereignty, then we have no guarantee that a single promise of God will ever be fulfilled...Maybe that one molecule will be the thing that prevents Christ from returning."[66]

How magnificent can God's sovereignty be if one loose molecule could threaten the whole thing? Though open theists would affirm that God is omnipotent, and therefore all created beings have power only within the boundaries he has set, those boundaries are wide and that power is real. This guarantees the eventual achievement of God's goals, while preserving the genuine freedom of created beings. God is able to direct genuinely free beings toward his goal for creation, which enhances, rather than undermines, divine sovereignty. Is a God that must control every movement of every molecule in order to bring about his intended purposes really a figure to be admired?

(ii) Predestination

In light of this understanding of divine sovereignty, open theology holds to a nontraditional view of predestination. 1 Peter 1:2 speaks of those "who have been chosen according to the foreknowledge of God the Father." Ephesians 1:4-5 reaffirms God's predestination—"For he chose us in him before the creation of the world to be holy and blameless in his sight. In love he predestined us to be adopted as his sons through Jesus Christ, in accordance with his pleasure and will."—as does Romans 8:29—"For those God foreknew he also predestined to be conformed to the likeness of his Son, that he might be the firstborn among many brothers."

The previous chapter presented an open theist's understanding of these passages of Scripture, and so there is no need to rehash the issue here. These passages refer to the predestination of a corporate group, not individuals. God has predestined the existence of a church, but he did not predestine individuals to attain or refrain from membership in that church.[67] The matter of predestination is not therefore a matter of foreknowing or determining the salvation of the individual, but rather the predestination of a divine movement giving rise to a corporate body known as the people of God. Whether or not the individual joins that corporate body is a matter of free will, not divine preordination.

(iii) Metasovereignty

In response to the attacks of classical theists, openness proponents emphasize the metasovereignty of God,[68] that is, God's sovereignty over his sovereignty. Open theists along with tradition theologians affirm that God is omnipotent. Therefore, as mentioned earlier, God could have chosen to create a world in which he exercised specific sovereignty, predetermining every event beforehand and knowing exactly what would happen from all eternity. God could have created a universe in which even the "free" acts of human beings were predetermined by him. He could have created a world that allowed him to remain immutable, impassible, and in possession of exhaustive foreknowledge of future events. Open theists adamantly affirm God's ability to accomplish all of this.

Through his metasovereignty, however, God has not chosen to create such a world, choosing instead to create a world in which he is engaged in a genuine give-and-take relationship with his creation in which events may occur outside or in contradiction of his will. He has chosen to create a world where he can be genuinely affected by his creation and in which free agents can disobey and shun him. He has chosen to create a world in which he does not exercise all the power, a world in which he must share the responsibility of forming future events, and a world in which he may suffer. The world is as it is because God sovereignly decided to create such a world. Open theology is the clearest exhibition, and not degradation, of the supremacy of divine sovereignty.

Practical Implications

Open theology has far-reaching implications beyond the realm of abstract theological and philosophical thought. The practical difference that such a concept of God makes in the lives of individual believers is immense. The Christian ascribing to open theology views prayer, providence, and the evil in the world much differently than the Christian ascribing to the classical model. By affirming this doctrine, the evangelical can accomplish one of the primary goals of the evangelical movement: cultivating a personal relationship with God.

Prayer

> Christians do not pray as passionately as they could because they don't see how it could make any significant difference. They pray, but they often do so out of sheer obedience and without the sense of urgency that Scripture consistently attaches to prayer.[69]

This is a tragedy. The traditional view of God facing an exhaustively settled future dilutes the biblical teachings of the urgency of prayer. Consequently, many Christians have such a distorted view of divine sovereignty that they fail to see any real purpose in prayer. "The common saying that 'prayer changes us, not God' simply doesn't reflect the purpose or the urgency that Scripture gives to petitionary prayer."[70]

Rather, prayer "is an activity that brings new possibilities into existence for God and us."[71] While prayer can never change God's final purpose for creation, it can alter God's plans for specific events along the way.[72] Indeed, the biblical testimony points to prayer as a determining factor in the formulation of the future, and God appears to bind "himself to this arrangement, even abandoning plans he'd rather carry out because people didn't pray."[73]

There is a giant gulf between popular, modern-day understandings of prayer within mainstream evangelicalism and the methods of prayer demonstrated by those in the biblical story. The resignation to the inevitability of "God's will" has led many to abandon the biblical view of prayer.

> In our efforts to pray it is easy for us to be defeated right at the outset because we have been taught that everything in the universe is already set, and so things cannot be changed. And if things cannot be changed, why pray? We may gloomily feel this way, but the Bible does not teach that. The Bible pray-ers prayed as if their prayers could and would make an objective difference....It is Stoicism that demands a closed universe not the Bible.[74]

Prayer demonstrates God's desire for genuine relationships with his creation. If he simply always provided our needs and fulfilled our desires without asking, our relationship with him would be distant, hidden, and impersonal. Prayer creates the "conditions necessary for God to be able to give us as persons what we need or desire."[75]

God wants to draw his people into his work to share in it. Prayer is a conversation, a demonstration of give-and-take relations between God and man. With respect to the formulation of future events, God has decided that the "routes into the future will involve a genuine divine-human partnership."[76] Indeed, in the "Hebraic understanding God is open and receptive to change...[grounded in] God's unrelenting commitment to be in a relationship with humanity."[77]

Providence

Open theism presents a view of providence quite different from that of traditional theology. If the future is eternally fixed within God's mind, as classical theology teaches, then the future must in fact be eternally fixed. If God does not see the future as a realm of various possibilities, then there must in fact be but one possible future. Consequently, there can be only one possible future open to us.[78]

We are like an audience viewing a movie for the first time—while we encounter the events depicted with uncertainty, there is nothing uncertain about the events themselves. They were fixed and settled long before we ever experienced them. Every inclination of hope toward one possibility or another reflects an illusion of the human experience as we helplessly endure wave after wave of inevitabilities.

Such an understanding of the future disinclines us from revolting against the evils of the present world, encouraging us instead to accept things as they are and events as they come. Of course, even this disinclination toward reform is inevitable, having been predestined by God. Indeed, any inclination we may have toward "changing" the future for the better reflects a preordained motivation and therefore does no such thing—because, after all, the future cannot be changed. I trust that how such fatalistic theologies may promote feelings of helplessness is clear.[79]

Those adhering to this traditional model of God often believe that they can do nothing to change the condition of the world because all things happen according to the will of God anyway. Consequently, many Christians do not grasp how destructive and terrible sin truly is, both in their own personal lives and in the world around them. They adopt a fatalistic view of the world, doing nothing to improve the situation.[80]

Richard Foster encapsulates the perverse understanding of reality such theologies can promote:

> A popular teaching today instructs us to praise God for the various difficulties that come into our lives, asserting that there is great transforming power in thus praising God. In its best form such teaching is a way of encouraging us to look up the road a bit through the eye of faith and see what will be. It affirms in our hearts the joyful assurance that God takes all things and works them for the good of those who love him. In its worst form this teaching denies the vileness of evil and baptizes the most horrible tragedies as the will of God. Scripture commands us to live in a spirit of thanksgiving in the midst of all situations; it does not command us to celebrate the presence of evil.[81]

Open theology better equips believers to understand the immense amount of power for good they can exercise in the world around them. The future is not a predetermined inevitability, but rather an ever-forming reality over which both God *and* human beings have immense influence. "Knowing that what transpires in the future is not a foregone conclusion but is significantly up to us to decide, we will be more inclined to assume responsibility for our future."[82]

This reality is particularly demonstrated through Old Testament narratives describing God's work and behavior. God is not interested in forcing his will upon preprogrammed automatons. Indeed, many conceptions of divine providence seem to correlate more to a child playing with her dolls than to genuine relationship.

In contract, the picture of God the Old Testament writers present is that of a collaborator, working with his creation to bring about his will.

God gives humans the "chance, if they will accept the responsibility, to contribute to a future that will be different from what it would have been, had they remained passive.[83]

Theodicy

How Christians and non-Christians alike understand the problem of evil has a tremendous impact on their view of God. According to traditional theology, God is all good, and so everything that happens, good or evil, must be a part of a greater good that we are unable to understand because of our limited perspective. After all, "The will of God is the necessity of things."[84]

The old Christian teaching to "[r]eceive the accidents that befall to thee as good, knowing that nothing happens without God" (*Didache* 3:10) is taken to mean that God orchestrates every tragedy for his greater glory. Even the most pious Christians, however, can struggle to understand how the Holocaust or the tragedy of September 11, 2001 could possibly fit into the meticulous plans of a loving God.

If, however, Christians understand the world according to the open theist view, it is easy to see how creation's misuse of free will could result in evil that is genuinely contrary to the will of God. Sin, and not God, is responsible for the suffering in the world. Just as God and his people are engaged in dynamic relationships of mutual influence, so also are God and his enemies—both sinners and the spiritual forces of evil—engaged in dynamic relationships of mutual influence.

Therefore, Christians should understand God as their helper, not their tormentor, in times of trouble. God allows the sin of free agents to run its course, though he is constantly working to redeem the evil sin creates. He is not the author of evil, and evil events do not find their source in the God of Scripture.

> Although God may sometimes bring about, or may deliver from, a particular misfortune, there is not a divine reason for each and every misfortune. Genuine accidents or unintended events, both good and bad, do happen, for that is the sort of world God established.[85]

God's giving free will necessitates that he must allow the consequences of those free acts. Yet Christians should understand evil, not as the product of the divine will, but as the result of a war raging between God and sin.[86] Since the cross, we have lived in the period between D-Day and the fall of Berlin. The decisive battle has been won. Victory has therefore already been secured, despite the enemy's continued resistance of the inevitable. "In the present structure it is not possible for God to allocate reward and punishment with strict fairness."[87] Such, however, will not always be the case.

Conclusion

A careful study of the philosophical and systematic theological implications of the open model of God in comparison with the thought driving traditional models reveals the real source of discomfort open theism inspires among traditional theologians. Open theism does not present any real threat to or stand in contradiction of evangelical theology. Openness is able clearly and consistently to affirm its own position and the distinguishing positions of evangelicalism.

It does, however, challenge the theological assumptions traditionally held by evangelicals. This is easy to understand considering the formative role the Reformed tradition has played in evangelical theology.[88] Openness does not challenge the evangelical view of Scripture. Rather, it challenges many traditional points of systematic theology common in evangelical circles. This does not, however, place it outside the evangelical framework.

Open theists stress the relational aspect of God in Scripture. This puts open theism in tension with other philosophical and systematic understandings of the nature of God but not with the biblical witness. The God of open theism and the God of Scripture is a God of relationship, a God who relates, a God who risks.

Open theism present a model of God that emphasizes genuine divine-human relationships, who is "open to the world and responsive to developments in history."[89] Human experience is not fixed from all eternity, a mere outworking of predetermined plans. Rather, it is an outworking of the continuous interaction between God and man. Our reality, and indeed our future, is imprinted with the image of a God who "interacts with us in our narrated, storied lives in a real reciprocal relationship," [90] a God who, in his love, not only affects us, but is in fact genuinely affected by us as well. While "God is unchangeable with respect to his character," he is "always changing in relation to us."[91] This is the philosophy of the open theist.

Endnotes

[1] Hasker, 131.
[2] Augustine, *City of God* 8.6, quoted in John Sanders, "Historical Considerations," in *The Openness of God* (Downers Grove, Illinois: InterVarsity Press, 1994), 80.
[3] Augustine, *Confessions*, 7.11.
[4] Hasker, 132.
[5] Pinnock, *Most Moved Mover*, 67.
[6] See Hasker, 132-33.
[7] Ibid., 130. These analogies do not offer dynamic, relational explanations for God's ability to change. The weather cannot always be trusted, a watch does not always keep the right time, and the changes of both are responsive to impersonal forces. The point of these analogies is simply to show that change often demonstrates quality without diminishing it, contrary to the presuppositions of Greco-Roman philosophy. 2:00 is no better or worse than 1:59, nor is spring superior to winter (at least not objectively speaking). These changes are quality-neutral changes, and so the analogies undermine Platonian presuppositions. Their direct application to God's character, however, is limited.
[8] Kaiser, 479.
[9] Hasker, 130.
[10] Anselm, *Proslogium* 7, quoted in Hasker, 130.
[11] Origin, *On Prayer*, in *Classics of Western Spirituality*, trans. Rowan Greer (New York: Paulist, 1979), 90-97, quoted in Sanders, "Historical Considerations," 75.
[12] A necessarily nuanced discussion regarding the legitimacy of the teachings of the Assyrian Church of the East are well beyond the scope of this book. For these purposes, I will limit my comments to say that I stand with the vast majority of Christian communities—including Protestant, Roman Catholic, Eastern Orthodox, and Oriental Orthodox—in accepting the conclusions of the Council of Ephesus.
[13] This is not to say that Christ had only one nature as taught by the Eutychian heresy; I do not advocate monophysitism. Christ still, of course, possessed both divine and human natures, as determined by the Council of Chalcedon in 451.
[14] Sanders, "Historical Considerations," 76-77.
[15] Fretheim, *Suffering*, 58.
[16] Stanely J. Grenz, *Theology for the Community of God* (Grand Rapids: Eerdmans, 1994), 85.

[17] Sanders, "Historical Considerations," 71.

[18] For a comprehensive defense of God's ability to change his mind from the perspective of those adhering to the traditional understanding of divine foreknowledge see J. Daniel Hays' "Anthropomorphism, Revelation, and the Nature of God in the Old Testament."

[19] Richard Foster, *Money, Sex, and Power* (San Francisco: Harper & Row, 1985), 20.

[20] Boyd, *God of the Possible*, 16.

[21] As discussed below, this is still the issue even if God's existence outside of time is conceded.

[22] Ibid.

[23] Ibid.

[24] Ibid., 16-17.

[25] Ibid.

[26] Ibid.

[27] Consider, for example, the title of Bruce Ware's book, *God's Lesser Glory: The Diminished God of Open Theism*.

[28] According to simple foreknowledge, God would be unable to alter the future because his foreknowledge of that future precludes the possibility of the existence of any other future. According to the Augustinian/Calvinist and middle knowledge model, God would be unable to alter the future because he has already predetermined it from eternity. Calvinism and Molinism (middle-knowledge) are able to escape the helplessness that the simple foreknowledge model throws upon God, but these two schools of thought run into their own problems in addressing biblical motifs discussed in the previous chapter. The God of Calvinism and Molinism has exhaustive foreknowledge of the future because he has determined all future events or manipulated all future events based on counterfactual, respectively. Simple foreknowledge teaches that God has exhaustive knowledge of future events, not because he determines them, but because he is able to gaze into the future. The merits of Calvinism and Molinism as opposed to openness is not relevant to the topic at hand. The drive of this book is not to demonstrate the superiority of open theology in comparison to other theological schools of thought, but rather demonstrate the compatibility of open theology with evangelical theology. Since these models are universally accepted as compatible with evangelicalism, they serve as a good comparison with open theism for the problem at hand. For a thorough discussion of the merits and drawbacks of all four schools of thought, see James K. Beilby and Paul R. Eddy, eds., *Divine Foreknowledge: Four Views*, (Downers Grove, IL: InterVarsity Press, 2001).

[29] Hasker, 149-50.

[30] Stephen Hawking, *The Illustrated A Brief History of Time* (New York:

Bantam Books, 1988), 14.

[31] Ibid., 14-15.

[32] Ibid., 13.

[33] Ibid., 34.

[34] Obviously, this section on time is an overwhelmingly simplistic rendering of modern scientific understandings. Theoretical concepts such as the finite but boundless nature of space-time (see Hawking, 145) or issues created by antimatter, black holes, and wormholes are well beyond the realm of this book's purpose and my own expertise.

[35] Ibid., 44.

[36] Ibid.

[37] Ibid., 28.

[38] Ibid., 32.

[39] "This is because there is a relation between the energy of light and its frequency (that is, the number of waves of light per second): the greater the energy, the higher the frequency. As light travels upward in the earth's gravitational field, it loses energy, and so its frequency goes down. (This means that the length of time between one wave crest and the next goes up). To someone high up, it would appear that everything down below was taking longer to happen" (Hawking, 43).

[40] Ibid., 43-44.

[41] Ibid., 156.

[42] Ibid., 38.

[43] Boyd, *God of the Possible*, 132-33.

[44] Hasker, 129.

[45] Keith Ward, *Divine Action*. London: Collins, 1990, 163, quoted in Terrance Tiessen, *Providence & Prayer: How Does God Work in the World?* (Downers Grove, Illinois: InterVarsity Press, 2000), 83-84.

[46] Hasker, 128. Open theists could argue that God is timeless in the sense that he exists outside humanity's understanding and experience of time. Divine timelessness here and throughout the remainder of this argument refers to the traditional understanding of divine timelessness, that is, God does not experience a sequential reality.

[47] Hasker, 128-29.

[48] Tiessen, 82.

[49] Augustine, *Confessions* 1.10.

[50] Sanders, *God Who Risks*, 208.

[51] Ibid., 211.

[52] Ibid., 212. See Calvin's *Institutes*, 1.16.2-3.

[53] Ibid., 213.

[54] Ibid.

[55] Augustine, *Confessions* 1.7.

[56] Sanders, *God Who Risks*, 213.
[57] Ibid.
[58] Ibid., 213-14.
[59] Tiessen, 75.
[60] Ward, 151, quoted in Tiessen, 80.
[61] Sanders, *God Who Risks*, 215.
[62] Tiessen, 85.
[63] Albert C. Outler, *Who Trusts in God: Musings on the Meaning of Providence* (New York: Oxford University Press, 1968), 96, quoted in Sanders, *God Who Risks*, 215.
[64] Sanders, *God Who Risks*, 234.
[65] Tiessen, 86.
[66] R. C. Sproul, *Chosen by God* (Wheaton, Illinois: Tyndale, 1986), 26-27, quoted in Sanders, *God Who Risks*, 234.
[67] Richard Rice, "Biblical Support for a New Position," in *The Openness of God* (Downers Grove, Illinois: InterVarsity Press, 1994), 56-57.
[68] I am indebted to Will Darr, a college classmate, for suggesting this term.
[69] Boyd, *God of the Possible*, 95.
[70] Ibid.
[71] Pinnock, *Most Moved Mover*, 46.
[72] Tiessen, 72.
[73] Boyd, *God of the Possible*, 97.
[74] Richard Foster, *Celebration of Discipline: The Path to Spiritual Growth*, 20th Anniversary Edition (San Francisco: HarperSanFrancisco, 1998), 35.
[75] Tiessen, 106.
[76] Sanders, *God Who Risks*, 66.
[77] Ibid. See Samuel E. Balentine, *Prayer in the Hebrew Bible: The Drama of Divine Human Dialogue*, Overtures to Biblical Theology (Minneapolis: Fortress Press, 1993), 268-69.
[78] See Boyd, *God of the Possible*, 93.
[79] See Ibid.
[80] Ibid.
[81] Foster, *Celebration of Discipline*, 194.
[82] Boyd, *God of the Possible*, 94.
[83] Gowan, 231-32.
[84] Hasker, 141 quoting Augustine.
[85] Sanders, *God Who Risks*, 216.
[86] For a more in depth look at this subject, see Greg Boyd's *God At War* and *Satan and the Problem of Evil*.
[87] Tiessen, 95.
[88] See Grenz, 80-81.

[89] Pinnock, *Most Moved Mover*, 41.
[90] Ibid.
[91] Ibid.

4 CONCLUSION

We have thus far examined the central tenets of both evangelicalism and open theism, assuming the former and viewing the latter in its best light. We must now turn to the central question of this book: Are open theism and evangelicalism compatible schools of thought? Knowing how evangelicals view Scripture and how open theists interpret it, can an individual legitimately claim the title of both evangelical and open theist?

Compatible Schools of Thought?

> We affirm the divine inspiration, truthfulness and authority of both Old and New Testament Scriptures in their entirety as the only written Word of God, without error in all that it affirms, and the only infallible rule of faith and practice.

This statement from the Lausanne Covenant poignantly sums up the distinguishing evangelical position. Open theology, neither explicitly through its positions or implicitly through logical contradiction, denies the validity of this statement. Adherents of open theism argue their position on strong exegetical grounds. Charges by critics that open theism is incompatible with evangelical theology are simply unfounded and unsubstantiated. Open theology is indeed compatible with and, in fact, driven by evangelical theological presuppositions. At no point does it conflict with the evangelical understanding of either the nature, purpose, or authority of Scripture as outlined in chapter 1 of this book. Why then the controversy?

Open theists have faced such an intense battle for acceptance within evangelical circles, not because their position contradicts evangelical theology, but because it contradicts theological presuppositions common within evangelical circles. The question, however, is not whether open theology is compatible with determinism, Molinism, or simple foreknowledge. Clearly, it is not. The question is whether open theology is compatible with the distinguishing marks of evangelical theology.

Often opponents of open theism find themselves unable to make the distinction and assume that, since open theology so radically contradicts their own personal theology and they themselves claim the title "evangelical," open theology must contradict evangelicalism. It is hard not to appreciate the irony of a conservative Protestant movement reacting violently against those who, on the basis of Scripture, question their community's deeply embedded traditional religious teachings. Indeed, the Evangelical Theological Society had its own Diet of Worms when it attempted to excommunicate prominent open theists.

Defining Systematics

The real issue here is a dogmatism that has developed around systematic theology. Proponents of both sides would be wise to recognize the difference between revelation and the organization of that revelation into systems. According to evangelical theology, the former is from God and without error, while the latter is open to human misunderstanding and fallibility. "Theology is nothing more than man's effort to rationalize God's biblical revelation,"[1] and both sides would do well to remember this.

N. T. Wright articulates well how the authority of a particular school of thought can unconsciously usurp the authority of Scripture:

> [E]vangelicals often use the phrase "authority of scripture" when they *mean* the authority of evangelical, or Protestant, theology, since the assumption is made that we (evangelicals, or Protestants) are the ones who know and believe what the Bible is saying. And, though there is more than a grain of truth in such claims, they are by no means the whole truth, and to imagine that they are is to move from theology to ideology.[2]

Many opponents of open theism within evangelicalism have correlated the authority of Scripture with the authority of their interpretation of Scripture. Consequently, when open theism challenges that interpretation, it is, to them, challenging the authority of Scripture itself.

At its heart, the debate is a clash of systematicians. The most ardent claim by opponents of open theology is that it limits God. This, however, is unfounded. Besides the various counters to this charge presented elsewhere throughout this book, this debate begs the question, can systematic theology adequately describe God at all? Doesn't reducing divine qualities to human theological systems itself limit God?

Systematic theology should not be held on the same level as revelation. Unfortunately, however, it often is, whether consciously or not. Systematic theology is simply the Christian's—particularly the evangelical's—best attempt to explain biblical revelation. God is infinite. In order to reveal himself in a way man can comprehend, he must, by logical necessity, limit himself, since revelation of an infinite God to finite man requires a finite manifestation of the infinite, which, of course, can never do justice to the fullness of divine glory. Therefore, every attempt to explain God limits him because man can only explain God in terms of his finite—and thus diminished—revelation of himself. Indeed, God's lesser glory is the glory he reveals to us.

Just speaking of God limits him because it restricts him to the confines of human vocabulary. To reach beyond this revelation is to reach into the infinite, which the finite mind cannot possibly grasp. God in his wisdom is perfectly capable of understanding what parts of himself man can understand and what parts of himself are beyond his grasp. God is a God who reveals himself in relationship and cannot be known outside his connection with humanity.

> In a sense, the relational description of God—speaking of the divine reality in terms of God's relationship to creation—is inevitable. We have no other vantage point from which to view God than his gracious condescending to us in what we call "revelation." However, God's primary concern in revelation is not simply that we be able to formulate propositions concerning his eternal being. God's intent is that we understand who he is as the eternally relational, triune God and who he is in relationship to the world he has made, in order, that we may enter into fellowship with him. Revelation, therefore, is the self-disclosure of God-in-relation.[3]

Consequently, open theists who claim their system describes God as he actually is, the ontological reality of his nature, fall into the same trap as the die-hard Calvinist. God as he actually is is beyond the grasp of mankind, and the very phrase "ontological reality of his nature" implies the circumvention of divine revelation. We simply cannot know what God knows. I regret that in writing this book I did not have time to explore the early Church's distinction between the divine essence and energies, as I believe it could shed some light on this debate. I must, however, leave this for another time.

Whether or not open theism corresponds to God's actual nature is not for man to know, for his actual nature cannot be known. To describe one system of theology proper as an ontological necessity is absurd. Open theism does, however, provide a coherent and clear explanation of revelation—as evangelicals understand the term—while maintaining the evangelical view of the authority and source of that revelation, and so it must be considered a legitimate expression of evangelical thought.

Stanley J. Grenz, in his book *Theology for the Community of God*, recognizes this danger of collapsing systematics into the revelation it seeks to systematize.

> As Christian theologians we are likewise faced with the temptation toward dogmatism. We run the risk of confusing one specific model of reality with reality itself or one theological system with truth itself, thereby 'canonizing' a particular theological construct or a specific theologian. Because all systems are models of reality, we must maintain a stance of openness to other models, aware of the tentativeness and incompleteness of all systems. In the final analysis, theology is a human enterprise, helpful for the task of the church, to be sure, but a human construct nevertheless.[4]

The debate over the legitimacy of open theism within the evangelical camp represents a move toward dogmatism with traditionalists in a sense affirming their own branch of evangelical thought as the only legitimate evangelical position. This is clearly a mistaken approach to the broad theology that is evangelicalism. Open theology at no point threatens evangelical theology but rather fits perfectly into the movement's foundational beliefs. The controversy is not the result of open theology itself, but of a group of evangelicals unable to distinguish their systematic interpretation of their source of authority from the authority itself.

Conclusion

Whether or not open theology is deserving of acceptance or offers the most biblically consistent presentation of the nature of God is a matter of debate. Its compatibility with evangelical theology as evangelical theology has commonly been defined and understood, however, should not be doubted. At no point does open theism contradict the basic tenets of evangelical theology, and so attempts to demonize open theists as not evangelically minded—particularly in the case of the Evangelical Theological Society's foolhardy attempt to expel John Sanders and Clark Pinnock—are unjustified and frankly incoherent. The evangelical community as a whole is not compelled to accept open theism, but for the sake of theological coherence and consistency, it must accept open theists as members of its own community.

Furthermore, the immense amount of effort poured into proving that open theists are not evangelicals distracts from the real purpose of evangelicalism: evangelism.

There is...an urgency about the way we go about our work. We resent unnecessary distractions; we resist unbiblical diversions. Can anyone believe that all other activities should be suspended until all Evangelicals agree on precise doctrinal statements? We certainly cannot. Hundreds of missionaries are looking to us to help them get the gospel to those who have never heard it. Scores of pastors count on us to analyze the mission of their congregations so that their growth will be encouraged. And, thousands of students look to us each year to equip them for ministry in churches, in cross-cultural overseas missions and in counseling clinics. To be truly Evangelical surely means more than debating about what Evangelicals are and who deserves the name. It means getting on with the Evangelical task. We are not a lodge carefully screening its members and briefing them with secret information. We Evangelicals are part of the church, grateful for our salvation and obedient to Christ's calling.[5]

Endnotes

[1] Herschel H. Hobbs, *Fundamentals of Our Faith* (Nashville, Broadman & Holman, 1960), 16.
[2] Wright, "The Laing Lecture."
[3] Grenz, 81.
[4] Ibid., 13.
[5] "Fuller Theological Seminary: What We Believe and Teach."

BIBLIOGRAPHY

Anselm. *Proslogium*.

Aquinas, Thomas. *Summa Theologica*. Edited by Anton C. Pegis. 2 vols. New York: Random House, 1945.

Augustine. *City of God*.

—. *Confessions*. Translated by Henry Chadwick. New York: Oxford University Press, 1991.

Balentine, Samuel E. *Prayer in the Hebrew Bible: The Drama of Divine Human Dialogue*. Overtures to Biblical Theology. Minneapolis: Fortress Press, 1993.

Batey, Richard A. "So All Israel Will Be Saved: An Interpretation of Romans 11:25-32." *Interpretation*, no. 20 (April 1966): 218-228.

Baum, G. *Is the New Testament Anti-Semitic*. Glen Rock, New Jersey: Paulist, 1965.

Boyd, Greg. "The Open-Theism View." In *Divine Foreknowledge: Four Views*, edited by James K. Beilby and Paul R. Eddy. Downers Grove, Illinois: InterVarsity Press, 2001.

Boyd, Gregory A. *God of the Possible*. Grand Rapids: Baker Books, 2000.

—. *Is God To Blame: Moving Beyond Pat Answers to the Problem of Evil*. Downers Grove, Illinois: InterVarsity Press, 2003.

—. *Satan and the Problem of Evil: Constructing a Trinitarian Warfare Theodicy*. Downers Grove, Illinois: InterVarsity Press, 2001.

Bruce, F. F. "The Letter of Paul to the Romans." *The Tyndale New Testament Commentaries*. InterVarsity Press and Eerdmans, 1963.

Brueggemann, Walter. "The Book of Exodus." In *The New Interpreter's Bible*, edited by Leander E. Keck, 675-981. Nashville: Abington Press, 1994.

Calvin, John. *Institutes of the Christian Religion*. Edited by John T. McNeill. Philadelphia: Westminster, 1960.

—. *The Commentaries of John Calvin on the Old Testament*. Edinburgh: Calvin Translation Society, 1843-1848.

Campbell, W. S. "Israel." In *The Dictionary of Paul and His Letters*, edited by Gerald F. Hawthorne and Ralph Martin, 441-446. Downers Grove, Illinois: InterVarsity Press, 1993.

Campus Crusade for Christ . "Campus Crusade for Christ Statement of Faith." 1998.

Childs, Brevard S. *The Old Testament in a Canonical Context*. Philadelphia: Fortress Press, 1985.

Childs, Brevard. *The Book of Exodus: A Critical, Theological Commentary*. Philadelphia: Westminster Press, 1974.

Chisholm, Jr., Robert B. "Does God Change His Mind?" *Bibliotheca Sacra* 152 (October - December 1995): 387-389.

Christianity Today International. "The Amsterdam Declaration, 2000: A Charter for Evangelism in the 21st Century."

Cottrell, Jack W. "The Nature of Divine Sovereignty." In *The Grace of God and the Will of Man*, edited by Clark H. Pinnock, 97-119. Minneapolis: Bethany House, 1995.

Cranfield, C. E. B. *Romans 9-16*. International Critical Commentary. New York: T & T Clark International, 1979.

Dunn, James D. G. *Romans 9-16*. Word Biblical Commentary. New York: T & T Clark International, 1979.

—. *The Theology of Paul the Apostle*. Grand Rapids: Eerdmans, 1998.

Durham, John I. *Exodus*. Word Biblical Commentary. Waco, TX: Word Books, 1987.

Enns, Peter. *Exodus*. The NIV Application Commentary. Grand Rapids: Zondervan, 2000.

Foster, Richard. *Celebration of Discipline: The Path to Spiritual Growth*. 20th Anniversary Edition. San Francisco: HarperSanFranciso, 1998.

—. *Money, Sex, and Power*. San Francisco: Harper & Row, 1985.

Fretheim, Terence E. "Divine Foreknowledge, Divine Constancy, and the Rejection of Saul's Kingship." *Catholic Biblical Quarterly*, Oct 1985: 595-602.

—. *Exodus*. Interpretation. Louisville: John Knox Press, 1991.

—. *The Suffering of God*. Philadelphia: Fortress Press, 1984.

Fuller Theological Seminary. "What We Believe and Teach." 2003.

Geisler, Norman L. *Creating God in the Image of Man? The New Open View of God—Neotheism's Dangerous Drift*. Minneapolis: Bethany House, 1997.

Gerstner, John H. "The Theological Boundaries of Evangelical Faith." In *The Evangelicals*, by David F. Wells and John D. Woodbridge. Nashville: Abingdon Press, 1975.

Gowan, Donald E. *Theology in Exodus: Biblical Theology in the Form of a Commentary*. Louisville: Westminster John Knox Press, 1994.

Green, Joel B. *The Gospel of Luke*. The New International Commentary on the New Testament. Grand Rapids: Eerdmans, 1997.

Grenz, Stanely J. *Theology for the Community of God*. Grand Rapids: Eerdmans, 1994.

Hasker, William. "A Philosophical Perspective." In *The Openness of God*. Downers Grove, Illinois: InterVarsity Press, 1994.

Hawking, Stephen. *The Illustrated A Brief History of Time*. New York: Bantam Books, 1998.

Hays, J. Daniel. "Anthropomorphism, Revelation, and the Nature of God in the Old Testament."

Heschel, Abraham Joshua. *A Passion for Truth*. New York: Farrar, Straus & Giroux, 1973.

Hillary of Poitiers. "On the Trinity." In *Nicene and Post-Nicene Fathers*. Grand Rapids: Eerdmans, 1983.

Hobbs, Herschel H. *Fundamentals of Our Faith*. Nashville: Broadman & Hollman, 1960.

Horne, Charles M. "The Meaning of the Phrase 'And Thus All Israel Will Be Saved' (Romans 11:26)." *Journal of the Evangelical Theological Society*, no. 21 (1978): 329-334.

House, P. R., and G. A. Thornbury, . *Who Will Be Saved? Defending the Biblical Understanding of God, Salvation, and Evangelism*. Wheaton, IL: Crossway Books, 2000.

Japan Bible Seminary. "Japan Bible Seminary Doctrinal Statement."

Kaiser, Jr., Walter C. "Exodus." In *The Expositor's Bible Commentary*, edited by Frank E. Gaebelein, 285-497. Grand Rapids: Zondervan, 1990.

Krause, H. J. *The People of God in the Old Testament*. New York: Association Press, 1958.

Ladd, George Eldon. *A Theology of the New Testament*. Grand Rapids: Eerdmans, 1974.

"Lausanne Covenant, 1974." International Congress on World Evangelization, Lausanne, Switzerland, 1974.

McCann, Jr., J. Clinton. "Exodus 32:1-14 ." *Interpretation* 44, no. 3 (Jul 1990): 277-281.

Minkoff, Eli C., and Pamela J. Baker. *Biology Today: An Issues Approach.* 3rd. New York: Garland Publishing, 2004.

Moo, Douglas. *The Epistle to the Romans.* The New International Commentary on the New Testament. Grand Rapids: Eerdmans, 1996.

Morris, Leon. *The First and Second Epistles to the Thessalonians.* New International Commentary on the New Testament. Grand Rapids: Eerdmans, 1991.

Moux, Richard J. *The Smell of Sawdust: What Evangelicals Can Learn from Their Fundamentalist Heritage.* Grand Rapids: Zondervan, 2000.

Murray, John. *The Epistle to the Romans.* The New International Commentary on the New Testament. Vol. 2. Grand Rapids: Eerdmans. 1968.

Origen. "On Prayer." In *Classics of Western Spirituality* , translated by Rowan Greer. New York: Paulist, 1979.

Outler, Albert C. *Who Trusts in God: Musings on the Meaning of Providence.* New York: Oxford University Press, 1968.

Packer, J. I., and Thomas C. Oden. *One Faith: The Evangelical Consensus.* Downers Grove, Illinois: InterVarsity Press, 2004.

Pate, C. Marvin. *The Reverse of the Curse.* Tübingen: Mohr Siebeck, 2000.

Pate, C. Marvin, J. Scott Duvall, J. Daniel Hays, E. Randolph Richards, W. Dennis Tucker, Jr., and Preben Vang. *The Story of Israel: A Biblical Theology.* Downers Grove, Illinois: InterVarsity Press, 2004.

Pinnock, Clark H. *Most Moved Mover.* Grand Rapids: Baker Academic, 2001.

Pinnock, Clark, Richard Rice, John Sanders, William Hasker, and David Basinger. *The Openness of God: A Biblical Challenge to the Traditional Understanding of God.* Downers Grove, IL: InterVarsity Press, 1994.

Quebedeaux, Richard. *The Young Evangelicals: The Story of the Emergence of a New Generation of Evangelicals.* New York: Harper and Row, 1974.

Rice, Richard. "Biblical Support for a New Position." In *The Openness of God*, 11-58. Downers Grove, Illinois: InterVarsity Press, 1994.

Sanders, John. "Historical Considerations." In *The Openness of God*, 59-100. Downers Grove, Illinois: InterVarsity Press, 1994.

—. *The God Who Risks: A Theology of Providence.* Downers Grove, IL: InterVarsity Press, 1998.

Schreiner, Thomas R. *Romans.* Baker Exegetical Commentary on the New Testament. Grand Rapids: Baker Academics, 1988.

Sparks, Kent. "The Sun Also Rises: Accomodation in Inscripturation and Interpretation." In *Evangelicals and Scripture: Tradtion, Authority, and Hermeneutics*, edited by V. Bacote, L. Miguélez and D. Okholm. Downers Grove, Illinois: InterVarsity Press, 2004.

Sproul, R. C. *Chosen by God.* Wheaton, Illinois: Tyndale, 1986.

Stott, John R. W. *The Message of Romans.* The Bible Speaks Today. Downers Grove, Illinois: InterVarsity Press, 1994.

"The Chicago Statement of Biblical Inerrancy." 1978.

Tiessen, Terrance. *Providence & Prayer: How Does God Work in the World?* Downers Grove, Illinois: InterVarsity Press, 2000.

Trinity International University. "Trinity International University Statement of Faith, 2000-2003. Statement of Faith for Trinity International University and the Evangelical Free Church of America."

Tyndale University College and Seminary. "Tyndale University College and Seminary Faith Statement." 2003.

Ward, Keith. *Divine Action.* London: Collins, 1990.

Ware, Bruce. "An Evangelical Reformulation of the Doctrine of the Immutability of God." *Journal of the Evangelical Theological Society* 29, no. 4 (442): 431-446.

"Westminster Confession of Faith." February 25, 2007. http://www.reformed.org/documents/wcf_with_proofs/.

World Evangelical Alliance. "World Evangelical Alliance Statement of Faith." 2001.

Wright, N. T. "The Laing Lecture 1989 and the Griffith Thomas Lecture 1989." *Vox Evangelica* 21 . 1991. http://www.ntwrightpage.com/Wright_Bible_Authoritative.htm (accessed September 2006).

—. *The New Testament and the People of God.* Minneapolis: Fortress Press, 1992.

Yancey, Philip. *Prayer: Does It Make Any Difference?* Grand Rapids: Zondervan, 2006.

ABOUT THE AUTHOR

Garrett Ham is an alumnus of both Ouachita Baptist University and the University of Arkansas School of Law, graduating *summa cum laude* from both institutions. Garrett currently resides with his wife and two children in northwest Arkansas, where he works as an attorney and serves as an officer and judge advocate in the United States Army National Guard. Additional information about Garrett and his writings can be found at www.garrettham.com.

Made in United States
Orlando, FL
10 December 2024